Promises Kept

PROMISES KEPT

The Life of an Issei Man

AKEMI KIKUMURA

Chandler and Sharp Publishers, Inc.
Novato, California

Library of Congress Cataloging-in-Publication Data

Kikumura, Akemi, 1944-
    Promises kept : the life of an Issei man / Akemi Kikumura.
       p. cm.
    ISBN 0-88316-563-5. — ISBN 0-88316-562-7 (pbk.)
    1. Tanaka, Saburo. 2. Japanese Americans—Biography. I. Title.
E184.J3K46 1991
973'.04956—dc20   91-22060

SECOND PRINTING 1997

Edited by W. L. Parker and Jon Sharp
Book designed bu Lisa Nishikawa and Jon Sharp
Cover design and art by Qris Yamashita
Composition by Page One Graphics / Lisa Nishikawa

Dedicated to the Memories of
    My Father
and of
    My Sensei, Hiroshi Wagatsuma

Contents

Acknowledgments

It took me almost a decade to finish *Promises Kept.* Over those years my son was born and my mother died; there were many events in between that kept me from completing this book. The support, encouragement, and spiritual sustenance that I received from friends and family helped me to continue my work and finally complete this manuscript.

I want to acknowledge several institutions that gave me funds for research. They are: The National Institute of Mental Health and the Institute of American Cultures, part of the Asian American Studies Center at University of California, Los Angeles. I also want to acknowledge the Japanese American National al Museum, where I am currently curating an exhibit on the Issei Pioneers in Hawaii and the Mainland, for the opportunity to be the caretaker of our Issei past.

I owe a great deal to the enormous generosity and patience of Professor Lewis L. Langness, who read countless revisions of this manuscript. Thanks also goes to Dr. Feelie Lee for the title of this book.

To my *sensei,* Hiroshi Watsuma, I owe my life-long profession as an anthropologist; to my family, sisters, brother, husband, and children I feel forever indebted; to my mother and father I owe my future, past, and present.

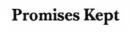

Promises Kept

Family Geneology

(Eldest to youngest siblings listed from left to right)

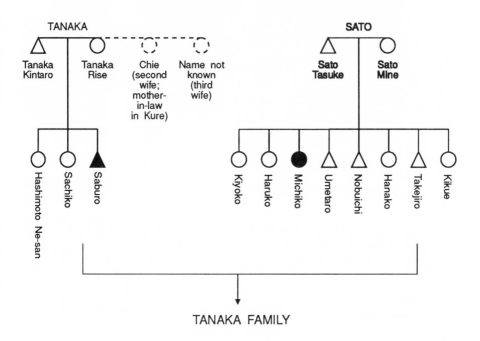

TANAKA

Tanaka Kintaro | Tanaka Rise | Chie (second wife; mother-in-law in Kure) | Name not known (third wife)

Hashimoto Ne-san | Sachiko | Saburo

SATO

Sato Tasuke | Sato Mine

Kiyoko | Haruko | Michiko | Umetaro | Nobuichi | Hanako | Takejiro | Kikue

TANAKA FAMILY

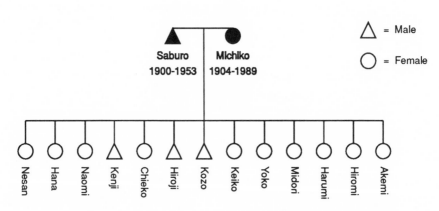

Saburo
1900-1953

Michiko
1904-1989

△ = Male

◯ = Female

Nesan | Hana | Naomi | Kenji | Chieko | Hiroji | Kozo | Keiko | Yoko | Midori | Harumi | Hiromi | Akemi

Introducing My Father and Our Family

As the youngest in a family of ten girls and one boy (two other boys had passed away before reaching four), I often felt as though I was born into a family entirely separate from the one that my older sisters and brother knew. They were privy to a past that they never shared with me, a time before the war when my parents played a more active role in shaping their children's individual and group identities by religiously teaching them various aspects of the Japanese culture. Every weekend they were privately tutored by Mama, who helped them perfect the complexities of the written Japanese language; and not a day passed by without Papa lecturing to them about Japanese history, values, and customs. But when the war ended, so did Mama's language instruction, and although Papa still continued to lecture, his speeches had lost much of the verve and intensity that they had before.

Many of the changes in our socialization stemmed from my parents' decision to remain in America which was largely shaped by the events that befell the Japanese Americans during World War II. On February 19, 1942, Executive Order 9066, signed by President Franklin D. Roosevelt and upheld by the United States Supreme Court, set the stage for the mass incarceration of over

120,000 West Coast Japanese (of whom sixty-four percent were American citizens), violating the civil rights and human dignity of an entire group of people based solely upon their racial ancestry. This single event dramatically changed the lives of all Japanese Americans, leaving a deep and irrevocable imprint, the effects of which continue to be felt generations later.

In May, 1942, my family was promptly evacuated to Stockton Assembly Center, where fair grounds were quickly converted into temporary housing quarters. Later, we were moved to Rohwer, Arkansas, one of the ten concentration camps hastily constructed by the government for people of Japanese ancestry. My family was one of the luckier ones, for in 1944 we received clearance to leave the confines of the camp with the understanding that we would farm in Arkansas and grow food to help the country in the war effort against the Axis powers. But many others stayed trapped behind barbed wire for the duration of the war.

Despite its impact (or maybe because of it), many of our elders chose to remain silent about the experience, making it difficult for following generations to uncover the past. They reasoned, "Why tell the children about it? It'll only hold them back." As one Nisei male told me, "We [Japanese Americans] are doing well now. Why bring up the past? It'll just rekindle racial antagonism."

Only recently has this sensitive topic been publicly aired. With the hearings of the Commission on the Wartime Relocation and Internment of Civilians established by President Jimmy Carter in 1980, we began to hear through the personal testimonies of the internees just how deep and longlasting the psychological and economic damages actually were and still remain for Japanese Americans. After forty years of silence, this was the first time that many of us heard our parents, our brothers, sisters and friends unlock secrets too painful to discuss before.

On August 10, 1988, President Ronald Reagan signed H.R. 442, the Civil Liberties Act, into law (Public Law 100-383), closing one phase of the long fight for redress and reparations. The Act acknowledged that "a grave injustice was done" and admitted the government's "fundamental violations of basic civil liberties and constitutional rights." The Act provided for "restitution" of $20,000 per eligible person and for "research, publication, and public educational activities." Moreover, it established that the evacuation and incarceration were: " . . . carried out without adequate security reasons and without acts of espionage or sabotage documented by the Commission, and were motivated largely by racial prejudice, wartime hysteria, and a failure of political leadership."

When I was growing up my parents never talked in specifics about their experiences in camp, yet I always suspected the importance that it played in my family's history because they always referred to the camps as a way of identifying people or events in the past. Marking their mental calendars with "B.C." or "A.C." ("Before Camp or After Camp"), they would say, "Oh, yes! That was 'Before Camp' when we still had our farm in Liberty," or "Wasn't that 'After Camp' when we moved to Little Rock?" And whenever they met a new acquaintance, they would ask: "What camp were you in?" Their answers must have said a lot because they would knowingly shake their heads and remark, "We were in Rohwer. Did you know the Yamagitas in block 27?" After running down a list of names, they would invariably hit upon one or two families that they both knew because although the Japanese Americans had settled throughout the Pacific Coast, we were a small, tight-knit community. Whether we lived in Sacramento, Fresno, Los Angeles, or Seattle, it was hard to escape the web of gossip, family ties, and community networking that bound everybody together.

It was in high school that I first started to question my mother about her experiences during the war. I had decided to write a term paper on the camps because in my history book there was only one sentence referring to the entire incident. It read something like this: "During World War II, the Japanese were evacuated into relocation centers for their own protection." I knew there was much more to it than that.

I pressed my mother for all the information she could recall, which, I might add, was not much. At first I was angered by her response, then later I was perplexed and disturbed. Since then, I have heard many Issei reveal similar thoughts. "Camp?" she said. "Ahh, yes. Those were good times, *neh?* Papa was never home to argue with . . . and my biggest worry—food and shelter—was taken care of." My immediate reaction was, "But how could you think of the concentration camp experience as a good time? You were locked up! Behind barbed wire! Your freedom taken away."

My father passed away before I had the opportunity to ask him the same question, but the camps must have been a great setback for him. He was forty-seven years old when he finally got released, starting out all over again as he did when he came to America in 1923, except this time he was twenty years older and had nine dependent children. He never talked about how the camps broke his spirit, instead he started to drink more, gamble steadily and, gradually, stopped talking about his past—Mama also stopped. I think both of them had given up on the younger children, resigned to the fact that they had lost us to America.

The war marked a turning point in my parents' lives as it did for many other Japanese American families. The economic and psychological losses were devastating and after the closing of the camps the Japanese Americans struggled to piece together their disrupted family and community lives and to regain their pride, dignity, and economic well-being. The postwar decades were spent working hard to achieve social and economic gains so that the children would be more accepted as an integral part of America.

But one of the costs paid for greater acceptance was a deeper cultural separation between the Issei and following generations of Japanese Americans (the Nisei and Sansei) and a subsequent loss of ethnic identity. In some families, children found it increasingly difficult to converse with their parents in Japanese. While parents spoke in their ancestral tongue, their children answered in English, and by the third generation, the grandchildren could no longer understand what their grandparents were trying to say. Even in the more traditional families like my own, Japanese customs and language gradually yielded to the accelerated process of Americanization.

When I was younger, I was glad that I didn't have to abide by the strict rules and standards imposed upon my elders. But as I reached adulthood and began to realize that social conditions had not markedly changed from the past, in that society still deemed me as foreign as my immigrant parents, the need to learn more about my cultural heritage grew stonger and the desire to bridge the discontinuity with my past became vital to my well-being.

During my last four years of graduate studies in anthropology at UCLA, I began to record the life histories of my mother and elder sisters and to piece together a comprehensive family history in my efforts to close the generational and cultural gap that I felt existed between me and my elders. With my mother I spent the most time, visiting her at least once a week and listening to her stories while sharing our meals together. Based on those interviews and a trip to Japan to meet my parents' relatives, I wrote *Through Harsh Winters,* a book about her life.

Throughout the interviewing and writing process it became increasingly apparent to me that truly understanding my mother's life and my family's history would require me to delve much deeper into my father's past. More than any event or individual in my family's history, he was perhaps the most influential in shaping the values and behavior of the entire family.

With that thought in mind, I started to write *Promises Kept* right after *Through Harsh Winters* was published in December, 1981. I thought the writing would come easily because I already had collected boxes of data on him while doing research on my mother. But the year I had given myself to complete the project slipped into eight.

One of the most difficult parts about writing was trying to find out exactly who Papa was. Some of those who knew him well refused to talk and others who were his peers were long deceased. My own memories of him were vivid but few since he had passed away when I was only nine years old. Therefore, to fill the gaps, many areas of his life were left to me only in my imagination and in fragments of information.

Before I started writing about him, and even when he was still living, my general feeling toward him was one of detachment. He seemed to be in another world very different from mine: his—very complex, impenetrable, and old; mine—very simple, accessible, and new. But another source of that feeling was the constant reminder from my elder sisters that we were Mama's children rather than his. To the younger children who grew up after the war (four of us), he had devoted the least amount of his time and attention. He used to remind Mama, while referring to us younger sisters and our upbringing, that "They're your responsibility—not mine." I guess he wanted to distance himself from the children who were more Americanized. He didn't want the blame for not raising us in the "traditional Japanese fashion." Whatever the reason, this label "Mama's children" followed us and became even more pronounced after his death. We younger siblings never disputed this comment, but it made me feel unconsciously as if Papa cared less about us, that he had given up hope, that being Mama's children instead of his somehow meant we were inferior or less loved.

After completing this book, I probably know more about my mother, brother, sisters, and myself than about my father. But what I did accomplish in the process of collecting, analyzing, and interpreting all the information about my father and trying to understand him, was a sense of belonging to his life. And now with prideful conviction, I could insist, "Yes, I am Mama's child, but I am Papa's child too!"

1
Papa

My father never talked to me about his dreams, Japan, his parents, and least of all, his failures. But he did share a lot of his inner thoughts with my older sisters and brother while they worked long hours together in the fields. That was when he was younger, when memories were fresher and dreams seemed more attainable. But for the most part, Papa was an enigma to me, an awesome, forbidding figure around whom I always felt very small.

About him clung a brooding aura of mystery and excitement that aroused my curiosity and provoked my imagination. Probably nobody around him was given the full liberty to see clearly all the facets of his personality for he was a man of many faces capable of bringing out the best and worst from those whose lives he intimately touched, simultaneously evoking laughter and sorrow, pride and contempt, pleasure and pain, respect and pity.

Although the time I had spent with Papa was short, the impressions he left were deep and longlasting. Occasionally, he would take me to find *yanagi naba,* a certain kind of edible mushroom that grew on the bark of willow trees near the banks of the river. The exciting part of this adventure was the knowledge that only certain kinds of mushrooms were edible; the others were highly poisonous, capable of instantly killing those who ate them. We had heard stories about families dying in Japan after feasting on a course of deadly mushrooms. But

Papa's discriminating eye could immediately spot the good ones from the bad. He always made the hunt exciting and I felt so privileged to be the one to go along with him.

When my sister Hiromi and I got elected to massage Papa's back, we both felt honored to be handed the job. That is, until it permanently became our chore. With clenched fists, I would pound up and down his back, sometimes using a short chopping motion by keeping my fingers together and extending them straight out. When I didn't have enough strength left in my hands, I would walk on his back, wiggling all my toes along his spine. We stopped only after he fell asleep.

Papa's back always seemed to ache; so did Mama's but she never made us massage hers. But I'm sure that every bone in her body must have ached after bending over all day picking the crops in the dry northern California sun. Hot baths and massages were partial remedies, but *moxa* (a cauterizing agent prepared from the leaves of a Chinese plant) seemed to be the only thing that brought them longer relief.

Papa was the expert. He knew all the right pressure points, the places to apply the soft mounds of herb. Just a pinch was placed on the right spot, then a match was lit. As the *moxa* slowly burned closer to the skin, Mama and Papa would let out a hissing sound, sucking the air in through their teeth, holding it, then exhaling it with one deep breath. It was hard to tell whether they were experiencing pain or pleasure.

The other occasions on which I could distinctly remember Papa were at community talent shows held yearly at the Buddhist Church. The older sisters would shrink down in their seats embarrassed because Papa would dominate the show. Besides being one of the singers, he also wanted to be the director and the emcee. Usually those positions were reserved for people of stature in the community. But I was proud of Papa, too young to know that he was breaking all the rules established by tradition. I knew that he was not like the others who appeared on the program. His voice sparkled loud and clear; he stood confident and relaxed, enjoying every minute that he held the stage. He was a real showman.

Other times with Papa were spent waiting and the circumstances surrounding those memories were the most vivid of all. Without any forewarning, I often found myself thrust into the back seat of the car to go into town with Papa. I guess I was like Mama's insurance policy. She thought that if I went along with him, he would not gamble. But my presence did not deter Papa when he had money in his pockets because he would head straight for the gambling den and leave me in the car. After two, three hours, I would begin to worry, wondering whether he had forgotten about me. But he always reappeared, sometimes with a Daddy Longfinger or a bag of jawbreakers to reward me for my patience.

The speedometer was the gauge to Papa's luck. When the needle quivered at eighty and the posts that divided the highway formed a solid white wall, I knew he had lost a bundle. "Papa, slow down," I would plead, but he would seem not to hear me, his eyes focused on a distant point somewhere beyond the horizon.

Was he thinking about the last hand he was dealt, or about the time when he was ahead and should have quit? Maybe he was feeling the last few coins in his pocket and wondering how he was going to meet next week's grocery bills? Or he could have been thinking about the inevitable argument he would have to wage with Mama and the excuses he would give her the moment he got home. Mama's nagging was incessant and the blistering arguments never ceased because as sure as the sun would rise the next day, Papa was going to gamble. It seemed like nothing could stop him—not Mama's nagging, the children's hunger, or any other threat.

It was two days after Christmas in the winter of 1955 when Papa finally met up with the only obstacle that would put an end to his gambling. Darkness had long claimed the sky and the evening dishes were cleared when a knock sounded at the front door. It was Sam, my eldest sister's brother-in-law. His ghost-white face trembled like a bowl of soft, white bean curd as he steadied his swaying body against the door jam.

"The boat capsized. Your father's still missing along with the others," he shouted. His father and older brother were among the others he was referring to. The wild look that glazed Sam's eyes was frightening, especially since he was a man who always kept his emotions well contained. He hurriedly left to return to his family, a rush of cold wind chilling the room as he closed the door behind him. I turned to the elders for comfort and reassurance, but their faces looked like masks, frozen by the fear of death. Mama was the calmest of all, sitting on the living-room couch with her hands folded neatly in her lap. She didn't cry. She didn't utter a word.

The clear morning sky had promised an exceptional day for fishing when my father set out with my eldest sister's husband, father, and son. By midafternoon, dark billowy clouds crowded the sky and gusty winds sent them rolling across the heavens, treacherously churning the waters of the San Joaquin River and suddenly capsizing the small wooden craft that all four had boarded.

Mama knew immediately that there was no hope although her calm demeanor did not betray her fear. But as for myself, I refused to believe that Papa was dead. He seemed indestructible, invincible, immortal. He made up all the rules of when to eat, sleep, work, and laugh. He seemed capable of defying all obstacles—the wind, water, bad luck—even death. He couldn't be dead, not unless he wanted to be.

Through the night the family lay awake, listening intensely after the passing of each car. I finally fell asleep certain that he would come walking through the front door proudly carrying a huge gunnysack full of sea bass, his clothes dripping wet and cold but his voice warmed with stories of how he defiantly fought with death and emerged the glorious victor after a long and furious battle. But when the next morning arrived deceitfully promising another day of gentle calm, I was to learn that they had discovered my father's frozen body curled into the fetal position in which he had entered the world fifty-five years before.

From that moment until the funeral everything seemed to move in slow motion like the dream sequence of a film. As I sat outside on the doorsteps listening to the muffled voices of elders huddling over funeral arrangements and discussing the family's immediate economic future, I suddenly had an urge to leap over the small pine trees that Papa had planted in the front yard several years ago. I stood up to take a running start but stopped short when I sensed the eyes of watchful neighbors and realized the impropriety that my actions would convey. As quickly as my urge had found me, came the uncontrollable stream of tears that blurred my vision of the neighboring houses. Those watchful eyes may have thought I was crying for Papa, but instead, my tears flowed from self-pity, from the realization that my life would never be the same.

The changes that my father's death would bring may have been welcomed by some of the elders who had had to live under his dictatorial rule; but for me, Papa represented stability and strength. Although conflict and turmoil rained on all of us when he was alive, I still felt deprived that I would never get to know him as an adult, that I would never share in the talks that he had reserved for the elders only.

Where did he come from? I knew he was born in Japan, but in what part? In my youth, I was too afraid to ask him; and besides, my interests were more concerned with the present than the past. As he carried me high in his arms, allowing me to view the world from his perspective, I found it hard to imagine that he too was once a child like me with elders whom he had to obey. He seemed to be born into this world with the authority and knowledge of an adult, an old soul who had lived a thousand lives before being thrust back into this life with our family. Clearly, he was discontented with the choices that the gods had made for him for he had grander schemes, higher aims and aspirations than the lot he was granted in his present life. Why would a man who was so fiercely proud to be Japanese emigrate to America and never return to his homeland? What reasons could have accounted for his quickly changing moods, his uncontrollable gambling habit, the demanding and stringent rules he imposed upon his children and wife? For answers to these questions and more, I sought those who knew him best: my mother, elder sisters, and my brother.

2

Mama

*M*y journey to unravel the mysteries of my father's past first began with my mother. Never did I expect her to be so eager to share with me her memories of the past. I suspect that much of it had to do with the circumstances of our lives at the time of the interviews. For the first time since coming to America, Mama did not have to work and had time to spare. Before her retirement at age seventy-two, she had always been too tired or too busy to engage in hours of leisurely conversation, leaving for work at six o'clock in the morning and returning home in the evening between six and seven, six days a week.

Occasionally, she would complain about the meager wages she earned and the dirty work she had to do while cleaning the forty odd rooms of the occupants in a dilapidated downtown hotel. But despite the low pay and the despicable working conditions, she approached her job with the seriousness of a law student studying for the bar exam. "How can I increase my efficiency and yet be more thorough?" she'd contemplate as she readied herself for the next day's work.

Many of the tenants were lonely Issei bachelors who didn't have any relatives in America. Eagerly, they would await the time when the key turned the lock of their door and Mama would enter to greet them with a warm smile because she would not only tidy their rooms but would also administer advice and concern, lend a sympathetic ear, and make their personal problems her own.

Every one of them called her "Mama," even though they were her generational contemporaries. To them, she was more than just a maid. She was also a psychologist, nurse, social worker, and mother all wrapped into one. To Mama, their needs and caring gave her distasteful work more meaning and joy. "Even in the midst of decaying matter, beautiful lotus blossoms grow," she'd remind me while referring to the occupants who called the hotel their home.

Once when I was still a teenager, I visited her at the hotel. Up the creaking staircase and down the narrow, dingy halls I tried to find her. "Ah, Tanaka-san? She's on the third floor," responded one of the tenants who showed me the way. At the end of a dimly lit hallway, amidst a mountain of dirty laundry, Mama crouched stuffing sheets and towels into large cloth bundles. Straightening her back to greet me, she proudly introduced me to the tenants who nosed their pale faces out from their dark cubbyholes to investigate the unfamiliar voice that intruded upon their space.

"Wait. I've got one more room to clean," she said, walking briskly down the hall where she stopped at a door, found a key in her apron pocket, and entered without knocking. On the bed lay an old Issei man smoking a cigarette, staring vacantly out the window facing Second Street.

"Ah, Mama-san. I was waiting for you," he said with a wan smile. Rising feebly from his bed, he steadied himself against the window sill, watching Mama as she changed his urine-stained sheets.

Mama sustained a constant patter of questions about his health and eating habits as she worked. Only after she made his bed, scrubbed his wash basin, and laid clean towels on the bed did she stop to look at him and administer advice.

"Have you been drinking plenty of water?" She asked sternly. The old man answered "yes" like a little child. "I'll leave a pitcher of water right next to the bed, so don't forget, *neh*. I'll check in on you before I leave," she said, turning to go.

The old man reached in his pocket and pulled out a dollar bill. It fluttered rapidly in his trembling hand. "You keep it," she insisted, closing his hands with hers.

I hurried to keep up with her as she trundled down steep stairs carrying the heavy bundles with her. "That man doesn't have long," she said matter-of-factly. "I think I'm the only one he has."

After that visit to her work place, I never again secretly took change from her coin purse. Although I knew her job as a maid couldn't be pleasant, I never realized how hard she worked nor did I imagine the neglected, dilapidated condition of the hotel and its tenants. I began to understand why she religiously patched and mended the aprons, the face masks, and the bandanas that she always wore while working. They were her protective gear, much like the sword and armor that a warrior used in battle.

"I have strong, sturdy legs. That's why I could work this hard," she boasted. But her legs were the first part of her body to disappoint her, forcing her to stop work after a lifetime of hard physical labor.

But even in her retirement Mama was never one to idle her time away. Poverty had long conditioned her to be a pragmatist, prodding her to engage in activities not for sheer pleasure but for their utilitarian purposes. Probably that's why Mama found the extra time and enthusiasm to talk to me about the past, knowing that what I recorded would eventually be compiled into a book and that its publication would help not only me but also the younger generations whom she felt had much to learn from the Issei experience.

When I first started questioning Mama about her life with Papa, she had nothing but praise for him. "Papa gambled but when it came to work, he was serious and responsible," she said. "He did his best, otherwise he wasn't satisfied. Me too, I'm very responsible when it comes to work. You know why? It's all because of Papa. That's what I learned from him. He would say, 'No matter what kind of work it is, you must do it with the thought that this work, no one can do it better—no one can beat me.'"

"Doing one's best" was a principle heavily engrained in each of us while we were growing up. As a child I could still remember Mama and Papa practicing their pear-packing techniques after working ten hours in the packing shed. With the evening dishes washed, the children watched as Mama and Papa sat at the dining-room table with squares of yellow-green wrapping to the left of them and pears to the right. With their hands in perpetual motion, they raced to see who could pack the pears the fastest and the neatest. After the race they discussed and analyzed the best method, the one that eliminated wasted motion yet retained neatness. Even when Mama worked as a maid, I remember watching her practice, over and over, how to make a bed with the greatest efficiency and neatness. "Think and work," she'd say, "And don't ever look at the clock."

Mama was also grateful to Papa for the strict disciplining that he meted out to the children. According to her, the children's good manners and discipline were qualities that were learned from Papa, not her. "Everyone raised by me is spoiled," she lamented. She was referring to me and the three sisters just above me in age. "Everyone raised under Papa is *shanto shitoru* [straight as a ramrod]."

Even her own disciplined behavior she attributed to Papa's teachings. "I'll tell you why," she said. "Papa never got up after the sun. I never slept in bed beyond the sun's first rays . . . Even the morning before he died, he said, 'Hey woman get up, wake up!' The morning was still dark but he insisted everyone wake up. He went to the children's rooms and woke them up."

The only fault that Mama was willing to find with Papa was his gambling habit, but even that she now condoned. "I couldn't blame him for gambling with all those children he had," she said wistfully. "He was always short of money . . . trying to make more by gambling. He could do anything even without money . . . Papa wasn't an ordinary man. He was a man of courage, smart . . . if only he didn't gamble."

I'm sure the twenty-three years that had passed since Papa's death had helped to dim her bitter memories. Besides, Mama was never one to dwell on the negative traits of others. But while he was alive, she lived in perpetual torment and anguish, always fearful about the family's economic welfare. Kenji (Mama's only living son) likened her situation to living in a haunted house. She never knew what horrors lurked behind each closed door. Papa could be cheerful and prosperous one moment, and irritable and broke the next.

I had often wondered why and how the two of them got married to begin with. They were as different as sunshine and darkness and as incompatible as fire and water. Neither could deny that they were totally unsuited for each other. Mama would bite her lips in silence when Papa would hurtfully remind her that he wanted to marry his brother-in-law's daughter from a previous marriage, an exquisitely beautiful and accomplished geisha who had an artist's spirit just like Papa's. She probably didn't dare to tell him that she should have married the even-tempered and dependable school teacher that her mother initially had in mind for her.

Papa admired women who were vain and flashy in their behavior and appearance, and Mama—being humble, self-effacing, and modest—was far from his ideal. Although he never allowed his daughters to wear make-up, he'd carefully demonstrate to them how they should apply it; how they should wear a kimono, comb their hair, walk with grace and dignity, and eat with delicate refinement.

After carefully scrutinizing Mama, he would criticize: "Why don't you put on a little make-up? Wave your hair. Make yourself more attractive!"

Mama would lower her head with hurt while fighting back the tears. "Why, if I had money to buy cosmetics, I'd get stockings for the kids. If I had money to get a permanent, I'd purchase shoes for the children."

Mama attributed much of their incompatibility to their differences in upbringing. Until coming to America, she had led a very sheltered, carefree, and comfortable life as a daughter of a wholesale sugar and flour merchant in Hiroshima City, whereas Papa—son of a farmer and born in a small village thirty miles outside the city—had experienced a childhood of suffering, raised by relatives who treated him like a nuisance.

Papa would often criticize Mama's parents and say, "Your parents never paid attention to the proper upbringing of their children. All they cared about was making money! They sent you to school, but what good did it do you?"

Mama said about Papa: "His thinking differed from mine. Me, I would listen to people and believe what they said. Him, he would say, 'Even if they say such a thing to your face, behind your back they are saying something else.' He would say things like that because he was raised by relatives. He grew up watching their faces, trying to figure out what they were thinking." Mama recalled: "Even when he was starved with hunger, he wouldn't ask for food. His cousin would get a rice ball for him and he hid in the storehouse to eat."

The circumstances of Papa's unhappy childhood were largely the fault of his father, who had decided to try his luck in America when Papa was only three years old. Leaving his wife and three children behind in Japan, he sailed away for the promised land in 1901. Like many of the early Issei, his father's intention was to stay for just three years at most, then return with enough money for an early retirement. But after three years ended and he found that he still had not achieved his goal, he decided to extend his stay. In the meanwhile, since he had not sent one word back to his family in Japan, his wife decided to remarry, leaving her three children, Papa and his two older sisters, to be raised like unwanted guests, shuffled from house to house, aunt to uncle, by whomever could momentarily house them.

Seventeen years later the first letter from America arrived calling for Papa to join his father abroad. By then Papa had left his small village and had found a job at my mother's family store. Papa's oldest sister had initially helped him secure the job, but once Papa set his foot in the door, his charm and wit carried him past the work area into the family room.

Mama didn't pay much attention to him—he was just a worker. But Mama's mother, Grandmother Sato, a shrewd businesswoman, instantly took a liking to Papa. She saw a lot of promise in the young man who could help the business grow even larger. He was bright, ambitious, and quick to learn, definite assets she wanted at her side.

The feeling of admiration was mutual. Papa respected Grandmother Sato for her intelligence and acuity for making money. She was a small woman, under five feet tall, who smoked long brown cigarettes and calculated figures in her head quicker than one could add on an abacus. All her children remembered her as the hardest-working person they ever knew. While she worked, her husband played, going out every night and sleeping until eleven o'clock the next morning. But she didn't seem to mind. She enjoyed running the business and making all the decisions, and he was quick to give her credit as the undisputed boss of the family, the one responsible for amassing the Sato family fortune. He was a kind man, generous to a fault with others, and an uncomplaining husband who allowed his wife to do just as she pleased.

When she heard about Papa's plans to go to America, she entreated, "Don't go. I promise there will be a place for you if you stay and help me expand the business." I'm sure that even as she made these promises, she wasn't thinking about him as a future son-in-law. In her mind, Papa was still a worker, a person who was below her social station in society. Instead, she was thinking in practical, business terms. Her husband was con-tented with the existing status and her three sons were still attending school and had little interest in the business.

But despite her using all the persuasive powers she could muster, Papa's mind was made up. Not only did he want to visit the strange new land, America, but he also saw this as a chance to see his father, the faceless man who had left such a deep and irrevocable scar on his mind.

On that long ship ride to America, Papa probably rehearsed over and over again the conversation he would have with his father. All the hate, the resentment of having been left homeless, would come spewing forth like pus suddenly released from a festering wound.

Caught up in his own predicament, he probably wasn't aware of the other *yobiyose* (immigrants who had been called by rela-tives) on board the ship, men who like himself were summoned by their fathers after many years of absence. But more than likely he took notice of the young picture brides who were sailing alone to America with photographs providing the only clue as to the physical appearance of their future husbands.

When the ship finally docked in San Francisco Bay, he along with the others were whisked off to the immigration detention station where they underwent inspection for hookworm, trachoma, and syphilis. Having passed the tests, Papa gathered up his bed roll and wicker basket and waited for his father's arrival.

"How will I know which one is my father?" he wondered while studying the faces of the men who lined the dock. Caught up with the strangeness of the new land, he soon forgot how uncomfortable he felt in his new Western suit; then, off in the distance, he spotted his likeness negotiating the crowd. His heart beat wildly and all the repressed hatred momentarily vanished as he watched his father approaching with the same curiosity that he himself felt inside. Although he had not seen even a picture of him since he was three years old, the kinship was unmistakable. And as father and son stood facing each other, there was silence, followed by the awkward moments of father trying to gain his son's good humor with inane remarks and son ignoring the shallow compliments of a guilt-ridden parent.

That night they checked into the Aki hotel. Though it was quite late, the lobby buzzed with the traffic of anxious husbands leading their shy picture brides up to rooms where they could consummate their marriages. The noise eventually settled, but Papa still could not sleep. The excitement of being in America waned in comparison to the bitterness he felt surging from within. He pulled up a chair next to the window and watched his father sleeping. The flickering light from the street lamp made the features seem to twitch in pain, as Papa slowly examined them. "So this is the bastard who made me suffer!" he thought to himself.

Suddenly, an uncontrollable urge swept over him. His entire body tightened into a knot as he tried to stand. Taking a step toward his father, he let out a deep groan, his fists violently shaking in the night. His father woke up with a start. "What's the matter, son?"

Papa stood there, his body still trembling. "Just a dream—a bad dream," he muttered.

"Go to sleep. We've got a long ride ahead of us tomorrow," the father grumbled, then turned over on his side and slumbered back to sleep.

Papa wiped away the cold sweat that had risen like tiny blisters on his forehead. At first, he hated himself for not finishing what he had started to do. But then he thought, "No. I won't kill him. I won't let the bastard off that easily. I'll make him suffer first, pay for all the misery he caused me."

The next morning they set off by horse and carriage for Liberty. I could only imagine what their conversation must have been like. Grandfather probably asked about his two daughters, his brothers, and other relatives in Japan, then the silence set in. As he watched his son from the corner of his eyes his yearning for home was rekindled. Now his son's youth and energy restored his hope of returning. In fact, that was why he had called Papa to America to begin with, to make enough money to go back home.

I suspect Grandfather wasn't a man who wasted many words. Instead, he silently scrutinized Papa's behavior, amused by his son's wonderment at the expanse of flat land that stretched before them, an occasional jackrabbit darting across the prairie offering the only signs of life for miles around. A feeling of well-being settled over him. He had imagined his son would be intelligent, astute—just like himself—and now he felt assured and relieved, especially since he had little time or patience to teach his son the ways of the new world.

"You learn by watching me," he told Papa when it came to pruning trees and doing farm work. "And listen closely," he admonished, "because I won't repeat instructions."

Those early days in America must have been some of the loneliest for Papa. At last he was with his father but he felt even more estranged from him than before. At times Papa tried hard to find redeeming qualities in his father so that he could put to rest the deep-seated resentment he now associated with a face. But what he saw was a cold, calculating, self-centered man who had little room in his heart for others, and no particular affection for a son he left others to raise. The only consolation Papa could find was the realization that the fatherly companionship and caring that he missed and longed for all those years were never within his father's capacity to give.

But despite the disappointment, Papa was still happy he had come to America. He was making money, twice as much as what he made in Japan. Conscientiously, he secreted it away in a cloth belt he kept strapped around his waist, even when he worked.

While Papa saved his money, Grandfather gambled his away at Takeyama-san's gambling hall in Japan town. Papa went along for the company because, on the weekends when work was over, the labor camp lay deserted as the men came to town to gamble, drink, and make merry. But long after most of them returned to camp, Grandfather would still be at the den, placing yet another bet. "Let's go home," Papa would urge. But not until his pockets were empty did Grandfather quit the table and call it a night.

Two years passed with the monotony of farm labor and weekend gambling blending one day into the next when the big chance that all Issei dreamed about finally arrived for Papa and Grandfather. Many farmers prospered that year, aided by the skyrocketing prices of the war's demand. With money that Papa had saved, father and son invested in a fruit crop and made approximately $50,000. Fifteen years later, farmers still remembered the huge fortunes that were made. "Your grandfather really made a killing that year," a Caucasian farmer used to tell Kenji.

Soon after, Grandfather Tanaka said to Papa: "Son, you're still young and strong, with many years of hard work ahead of you. You stay in America. Find your own way—like I did. Meanwhile, I'll go home—invest this money for you. There will be a place waiting when you come home." Mockingly, he laughed. "If you have any wits about you, you'll return a rich man like me." With those departing words, his father left Papa stranded with only a few dollars in his pocket.

"That son-of-a-bitch!" Papa shouted. "He's done it again. But this time he's leaving me in America." For the next few days, Papa spent all of his time in the Miyajima gambling den, drowning his rage in *sake* (rice wine), pampered by the barmaids who helped him gamble away the last cent left in his pocket.

When his head cleared and the smell of putrid *sake* stopped seeping from his pores, he reluctantly set out for San Francisco, persuaded by a friend who had convinced him that he should see his father off at the docks. As the ship slipped out of the harbor, he cursed: "Beast! Devil! With my sweat and toil you leave! I'll show you. I don't need to depend on you for anything!"

Papa's father returned to Japan and bought land in his own home village: seven and a half acres of mountainous land packed with cedar trees. Next he went about finding a suitable wife for his son. His eldest daughter insisted that Sato Michiko would make an excellent choice. Her parents were long established, reputable merchants in Hiroshima City and Papa already knew her since he worked for the Sato family before going to America. She had a good disposition (cheerful), was educated (four years of girls' middle school), healthy (she could bear a lot of sons), attractive (fair skinned), and filial (she would look after her in-laws in old age). What more could a family ask for in a *yome-san* (daughter-in-law)?

Initially, Mama's mother was not in favor of the proposal. She liked Papa, but never thought of him as an equal. After all, what kind of family would allow their *chōnan* (eldest son) to work for another as a common laborer? Grandmother Sato would not have been so impolite as to express her thoughts directly, but instead she probably boasted about the Sato family line, long established as merchants in Hiroshima City.

Grandfather Tanaka allowed her to complete her thoughts, his mouth bent in a crooked smile. "Come to Takata. See for yourself," he suggested, radiating an air of superiority.

Grandmother Sato accepted the invitation, taking Mama with her, traveling further into the countryside than either had ventured before. The reception was elaborate and Grandfather

Tanaka proved to be quite a generous and gracious host, but what impressed Grandmother Sato the most was the land that Grandfather Tanaka had recently purchased. "Their wealth may be new," she thought to herself, "but with this much land packed with cedar trees, my daughter would never have to worry about money." And of course Saburo, as the only Tanaka son, would inherit all the land. By the time she left the Tanakas', there was no doubt in her mind that he would soon have Michiko as his daughter-in-law.

The wedding arrangements were set. Papa returned to Japan, summoned by his father, to discover that he was to marry Michiko, the Sato's second eldest daughter. She would not have been his choice but apparently he did not protest the arrangement. Maybe he saw Mama as an asset, a bride whose family he could possibly turn to if things should turn sour with his father. And if the marriage was unsuccessful, he could always lay the blame on his father, who had arranged it.

No sooner did Papa settle in with Mama than the bickering began between his father and himself. At night, after everyone had gone to bed, he would tell his new bride: "Ha! He thinks he made all that money by himself. But if it wasn't for me, he would still be in America. *Broke!* It was with money *I* saved that we made that big score. He gambled all his earnings away!"

She would patiently listen to her husband's diatribe, then she would demurely suggest, "Why don't we go to America? Get away from this bickering?" She had always wanted to see foreign countries, experience the unknown. In fact, that was her reason for marrying Papa. His father's wealth didn't impress her. It was America and its aura of excitement that attracted her. She knew Papa could guarantee adventure.

As the arguments between father and son grew more violent, her quiet urgings became nightly pleas: "Let's go. Let's stay just for a while. You'll feel better when we come back. Please. Let's go to America."

When Papa finally agreed, Mama sold some of her finest silk kimonos to pay the fare. Reluctantly, they broke the news to both parents. Grandmother Sato kept pleading with them not to go, and Grandfather Sato had similar advice: "America is not such a good country. Your future is here." But, borrowing money from both parents, they left from Yokohama, bound on the *Korea Maru* for America. Neither of them would have guessed, as they watched the land disappear over the horizon, that it would be the last time they would ever see their homeland.

3

Visit to Takata

*F*ifty-seven years later, I was the first one in my family to go back to see my parents' families. The arrangements were made. I would stay with my mother's eldest brother. He was *honke*, head of the main household, the one who inherited the family business. The main purpose of my trip was to learn more about my mother and her family background. But since I would be staying in Hiroshima for quite a while, I was determined to locate my father's family and to visit his village. Maybe then I could fill in many of the gaps in my father's past that eluded me.

My mother insisted that I not go: "They will think you are after the family wealth. As the only son, Papa should have inherited all the land that his father bought. Believe me, they will not welcome you, so don't go!"

When I pressed my mother further, she began to reveal stories I had never heard before. She told me that the money they had borrowed from her mother and Papa's father was never returned because of Papa's gambling habit. The last time that they heard from Papa's father was when she had written a letter asking if she could come home with the children. She and Papa anxiously awaited the response to their letter but when it arrived it was devastating: "Know shame! Never a letter or a cent for six years and now you want to come back! You are no longer children of mine. Do not set foot on this soil again!" How ironic that

Grandfather Tanaka could not forgive his own son for the same thing he had done to his young family years earlier. That was the last time they heard directly from Papa's father. Through a distant relative word came that Grandfather Tanaka had married again, this time to a woman who had two children from a previous marriage. He wanted Papa to know that he had willed part of the land to these children, but that the prime, best parcel would be set aside for him.

Less than two weeks after I arrived in Hiroshima, I could not contain my curiosity. I convinced my cousin Shōsō-san (my mother's eldest brother's first son) to take me to Takata, my father's village. At first, he reluctantly agreed. But after I gave him more background about my father's family, he too became curious. I was elated because without him, I couldn't have done it. He was my translator, chauffeur, research assistant, secretary, brother, and friend.

Later, Shōsō-san confessed to me that he would not have taken me to Takata unless he was absolutely certain that I had not come back to reclaim Papa's share of the land. "In Japan the biggest family feuds involve inheritance and how the parents' property is divided," he said, and Shōsō-san didn't want to be a party to that.

We followed the Ōtagawa River that flowed into the Honkagawa. On either side of the river sloped a range of mountains, heavily wooded with pine, bamboo, and small maple trees. The villages lay nestled between the mountains along the river banks, and as we traveled further away from Hiroshima the river narrowed and the villages became even more scattered. The undisturbed beauty of the land and the age-worn houses made me think that not much had changed since my father was here. And if he had been returning with me, he probably would have recognized familiar landmarks like a bend in the river, the widening of the valley's gorge, the different shapes of mountain ranges. Luckily, the atomic bomb did not deface the countryside as it had the city.

We passed Mugi-cho, then Ugi-cho, and stopped to ask two young boys the directions to Takata. "It's just up ahead," they pointed. "To the left is a blue bridge—take it and you'll find Takata."

Upon crossing the bridge, we stopped at the largest building in the village, a grocery store. When we entered, Shōsō-san did all the talking for me. He told the two women in the store that I had come from America and wanted to talk to Tanaka Seizo, my father's cousin and his only living relative. I hastily pulled out my calling card (an essential source of identification and introduction in Japan) and presented it to the younger woman, who was apparently the storekeeper.

She carefully scrutinized it, looked at us suspiciously, then hesitantly introduced herself: "I'm Atsuko—the eldest daughter of Tanaka Seizo. My father isn't home now, but I expect him back shortly." She was a thin, attractive woman who appeared to be in her early thirties. Her tense, unfriendly demeanor made me feel uncomfortable. I looked at Shōsō-san, wondering what to do next, when she untied her apron and asked us if we would like to wait for him. We nodded in agreement and followed her into the house that adjoined the store in the back.

She led us into a large sitting room with sliding screen doors drawn wide open, revealing a calm and breathtaking view of the village. A sea of lush green rice stalks, rising four inches high, crept close to the edge of the house, gently swaying in the morning sunlight. In the distance, about a hundred yards away, the mountainside rose dramatically covered with a thick green quilt of pine, bamboo, and maple trees. I wondered if Papa had decided to come back to Takata to live, would I be living in one of the houses I now gazed upon? And maybe the same strained look that marked Atsuko's face would be mine as I struggled to live harmoniously under a single roof with three generations.

I think even Shōsō-san was taken in by the tranquil beauty that lay before us. He was a workaholic, like his grandmother, thriving on the daily pressures, challenges, and demands of running his own business, and only a rare occasion like this one could have pulled him away in the middle of the week to sit in the quiet of the countryside. I felt truly privileged to have his company.

While we waited for Seizo-san I explained to Atsuko the reason

I had come to Japan. I tried to reassure her troubled mind that the Tanaka family was doing quite well in America and that I did not return to claim any property rights. Slowly her demeanor changed, her serious, stern expression relaxing into youthful curiosity. Only then did she decide to offer me fragments of information she remembered about my grandfather.

"He was quick tempered," she said. "And he was left-handed." What a curious set of characteristics to remember about a person, I thought to myself. Both of them were uncomplimentary, outside of the norm, but maybe that's what Grandfather Tanaka was in this small village: a deviant.

Very few in his village had left for America, and fewer still had returned with as much money. Mama told me that his knowledge of English made him the official village translator, the expert on America and things foreign, and when visitors came to him for advice or insight, he played his part to the hilt, relying on his props—a cup of American coffee, a smattering of English words, a memento from America—to authenticate his unquestioned authority.

When it drew closer to lunch and Seizo-san still hadn't returned, Shōsō-san and I excused ourselves and said we would come back in several hours. We didn't want to overextend our welcome, knowing that if we stayed we would put Atsuko in the awkward position of having to offer us lunch.

We took a short thirty-minute ride to the waterfalls of San Dan Kyo, where we ate lunch, took pictures, and watched young lovers walk hand in hand. Did Papa come here often, I wondered, long before the tourists discovered its irresistible mystery? Did he fish in these streams and know the paths I was walking? Did he dream about this place when he was picking grapes in the hot, arid, flat lands of Central California, where nothing stirred but the heat waves rising from the valley floor?

By two o'clock we were back at the Tanaka residence. Atsuko greeted us at the door, a little more cheerful than before. "My father is home now and waiting for you," she said. She led us to the same sitting room and motioned for us to sit next to the Buddhist altar. It was the most elaborate one I had ever seen, gilded, seven feet high and four feet wide. Shōsō-san whispered, "You rarely see such a fancy one even in Hiroshima. This family must cherish their ancestors."

There we settled on the straw mats, curiously looking about at our surroundings when Tanaka Seizo entered. I had the feeling he had timed his entrance like an actor, first making us wait in anticipation, then entering when the spotlight focused on him. Shōsō-san straightened his posture and both men bowed deeply, muttering honorific greetings that I could not fully comprehend, touching their heads to the straw mat with each bow. Seizo-san's wife, a stout, plump woman with red cheeks, pinched lips, and eyes smaller than black beans, entered next and repeated the same ritual.

I could not take my eyes off Tanaka Seizo. He looked like a reincarnation of my father: high cheekbones, deep-set piercing eyes, tall chiseled nose, and thin lips. He appeared to be about five feet ten inches tall, lean, and agile. Seizo-san was my father's cousin, the second son of Tanaka Chiyotaro, who was my grandfather's older brother.

His skeptical look prompted me to quickly produce my calling card, and while Shōsō-san explained to him the reason I had come to Japan, he carefully studied my appearance. I tried to avert my eyes, looking down at the mat to allow him to freely observe me. A sidewise glance out of the corners of my eyes caught a calm expression on his face, but his rhythmic tapping of my calling card against the wooden table top betrayed his apprehension.

Atsuko's husband, an adopted son, came home shortly after making store deliveries and inquisitively joined the others who sat watching my every move. As we sipped Calpis (a creamy, sweet drink) and nibbled on the dried codfish served by Atsuko, I began to reveal more of myself and my reason for coming to Japan. They all listened attentively, especially Seizo-san, who became more animated as my story progressed.

"The mountain and land that your grandfather bought was squandered away by his wife and himself," he casually remarked. Evidently my grandfather liked to drink and gamble just as had

my father. Mama had told me that much about him, yet the
nonchalant and cavalier manner in which Seizo-san offered this
information made me suspect that he was not telling me the
whole truth, especially since his general approach to me was very
guarded.

"Your mother and father stayed about three nights in Takata
before leaving for America," he continued. "I remember your
mother. She was a very studied, educated person. Your father—
he was tall, good at singing *Namu Yabushi* and old traditional
songs." These glimpses of the past were all the information he
chose to offer, his face revealing more than his words.

"See that picture," he said, pointing to a frame above the
sliding paper door. "That's your grandfather." The deep,
penetrating eyes looked down at me, making me feel uncomfortable. "So this is the stinking bastard that made Papa suffer," I
thought to myself. He looked just like my father, except his face
was not quite so long, his cheek bones were higher, his nose
slightly broader, and his eyebrows shading deeper set eyes.
Mama had told me that after returning to Japan he had become
frightfully religious, going from temple to temple, day after day.
But I couldn't detect a trace of repentance or enlightenment in
the cold, penetrating eyes that made me shiver in the warm
afternoon sun. I wanted to ask him, "What really happened to
all that money? Did the house we sit in belong to him at one
time? Is that why his picture still graced this living-room wall?
Was the land we gazed upon once Papa's? Why was he so
unforgiving with his son? Why did he exile his son in a land that
he himself never wanted to make home?"

We later walked to the site of my grandfather's grave. In the
same grave was Mas-san, his youngest daughter (my aunt), who
never married. The grave site was nestled on the side of the
mountain, the graves clustered closely together, theirs being the
most visible since it was the largest and newest one, made of white
marble. She had died recently, March 3, 1977, several months
before my arrival. "If only I had come sooner!" I thought to
myself. She would have answered my questions, told me about
Papa's childhood, his mother and father. Mas-san was the one

who cared for my grandfather until his death. I didn't know what happened to his second wife; nobody made mention of her resting place, but I assumed that it was Mas-san who remained the closest to him because she was the one who shared his grave.

Shōsō-san later told me that if my father's ashes were returned to Japan, they would be placed in the same grave with his father and sister. He also surmised that the fancy Buddhist altar and the elaborate tombstone must have been paid for by money that Mas-san had saved. I agreed with him that she must have had some money saved after working for twenty years and remaining single all her life, and that Seizo-san must have inherited her money since he was her closest living kin.

We walked further up the mountain and across to another grave site. There lay buried some more of Papa's relatives, all of whom had died during the war. One was the grave of my father's real mother. Mama had told me she had remarried and left the village. I wondered what circumstances led her back to Takata? And what was her relationship like with her spinster daughter and her husband who had remarried? As we walked through narrow mountain paths, past the rice fields and small thatch-roofed houses, I could picture my father in this village, a place too small to hold his dreams, too isolated to satisfy his curiosity. It seemed inevitable that he, like his father, would someday leave.

The village at its largest accommodated eighty households; when my father lived there it had sustained sixty-three households and now there were only forty-four. For hundreds of years the villagers farmed rice and mushrooms, traveling by boat to Hiroshima to sell their products in the marketplace. Most of its inhabitants were somehow related to one another, the villagers of Takata proudly claiming that they were descendants of the Taira warriors. According to village lore, the Taira clan, who claimed to be descendants of the Imperial family, took refuge in the mountains of Takata after their crushing defeat by the Minamoto clan in A.D. 1185.

We left the Tanaka household at six-thirty—just before dinner. We probably stayed longer than we should have, but the unsettled feeling I felt inside made me want to linger. Shōsō-san checked his watch, indicating to me that it was time to go, and Seizo-san immediately picked up his cue. "Come again," he offered politely. I thought his invitation was genuine.

My last weekend in Japan Shōsō-san asked me, "Where would you like to go the most?"

"Takata," I said. "I don't know when I'll be returning, and when I do, I doubt whether I'll go and visit the Tanakas."

As we drove slowly in the rain, I treasured the unforgettable panorama that unfolded before me through the raindrops: the mist clinging to the mountainside; the lush green color of the rice fields; the lacy bamboo jeweled with glistening raindrops; the two-storied houses with blue or brownish-red tile roofs; the smell of burning wood; the narrow roads with deep gutters on either side; the ubiquitous schoolchildren dressed in dark navy blue skirts or pants and white shirts; the people walking or riding bicycles wherever we traveled; an occasional male urinating by the roadside; the small graveyards cradled on the side of the mountains, and the rivers that flowed everywhere around Hiroshima.

The last visit to Takata was even less ceremonious than the first. Atsuko and her husband stood outside the store talking to Shōsō-san and me, without inviting us into the house. "Come and visit us again when you are in Japan," they mentioned as an afterthought when our conversation seemed to lag. I smiled politely and bade farewell, knowing that I would probably never see them again.

As we headed back to Hiroshima, I sat in silence, feeling removed from my body and thoughts. "Too bad you didn't return to Japan sooner when Mas-san was still alive," Shōsō-san commented regretfully, trying to brighten my quiet mood. "You would have received a warmer welcome since she was your paternal aunt."

But the tepid reception that I had received from the Tanaka family was not what disturbed me. I left Takata knowing that my father's early past would forever remain a mystery for it now lay buried deep with the spirits of the dead, and what was still in the minds of the living would never be revealed—at least not to me.

4

Keiko

*I*mmediately after returning from Japan, I called my sister Keiko (fifth eldest daughter), who lived in Sacramento, to ask her if I could come and spend several weeks with her. The enthusiasm and memories of my trip were still fresh and I didn't want to wait too long before committing myself to writing. I also wanted to visit my two eldest sisters who lived nearby; through their combined life stories, I felt that I could begin to weave together a clearer picture of the family's early history with Papa.

Keiko, who was ten years my senior, was the sister whom I remembered most vividly. The rest had married and left the household by the time I was seven years old. Keiko was right in the middle of the birth order. There were four sisters and my brother who were older than she, and five sisters who were younger. She rarely talked to me, or for that matter, even looked at me, the decade that lay between us separated our interests, our thoughts, our dreams.

Yet I idolized her from a distance, always eager to win her attention. A few times I did, although on one occasion that I distinctly recall it was totally unwelcome. One hot summer afternoon when I was about nine years old her watchful gaze came to rest on the nape of my neck. She pushed aside my long hair and looked at me with disgust: "When was the last time you took a bath?"

"Last night," I blushed.

"Go draw a bath and call me when it's ready. I'm coming in to scrub you down," she ordered.

I must have spent an "eternity" of about thirty minutes cleaning the tub, slowly filling it with water, finding another excuse to stretch the time before I called her in. I was just entering puberty, my breasts just hinting at the onset of womanhood, and I was embarrassed to have her see me naked. Nobody did. Not even Mama. "Ready," my voice squeaked as I sank deeper into the water trying to hide. She marched right in and started to scrub my neck briskly, her perfunctory manner slowly easing my embarrassment.

Despite her apparent indifference toward the younger sisters, I knew she really cared. I first realized as much when she bought Hiromi (ninth eldest daughter) and me a new pair of roller skates. "Here. I bought something for you kids," she said, casually laying the two boxes on the dining room table without any fanfare. Hiromi and I were overjoyed because we rarely received gifts that were not essential to our immediate survival. But more than anything else, we were elated to discover that Keiko thought enough about us to spend her hard-earned wages on us. That was the ultimate sacrifice for Keiko because, after helping Mama with all the household bills, she hardly had enough left over to spend on her biggest weakness: clothes. Keiko had quite a flair for fashion. To save money, she would sew most of her own clothes and she bought accessories to give her outfits a finished look.

As a young girl I always wanted to look like her. I would quietly admire her as she studied each feature in the three-way mirror, her face resting between her palms. Then with the nails of her forefinger and thumb, she would deftly curl her long, thick black lashes, her lids fluttering like wings with each flick of the nail. Secretly, I would try to perfect the same skill, but each time I would only manage to yank out a few more lashes. After she had each lash sweeping up with just the right curvature to frame her large, doe-shaped eyes, she would apply strawberry red lipstick, first to her upper lip, beginning at the corners and stopping at the center, then to her lower lip with one slick motion. Blotting her lips on tissue paper, she would lean back on the stool and squint in the mirror to examine her art work and add the finishing touches: a pinch on the cheeks, an extra blot of the lipstick and an uplift of the eyebrows with her forefingers. I used to think to myself, "She looks just like a dark-haired version of Janet Leigh or a friendlier, less sophisticated Jean Simmons."

All the boys seemed to be enthralled with Keiko, but only the brave dared to come over the house when Papa was still living. He could spot them through our kitchen window driving their cars up the dirt roadway. And before they could reach the house and get out, Papa would be waiting for them, wielding a baseball bat like a samurai sword, cursing at them in Japanese as they took off without coming to a stop. Keiko would run to her bedroom and bury her face in the pillow, embarrassed by Papa's behavior, afraid to face his fierce temper.

"None of my girls are allowed to go out on dates," he'd yell. "And take that lipstick off. You look like a whore."

When Papa died, a green light flashed for all the boys to come calling. Keiko soon settled on Ted, a Nisei, second generation, American-born Japanese from Sacramento who came from a family of impeccable standing in the community. What Mama liked most about him was that he held a steady good-paying job as a draftsman. He was just the opposite of Papa: soft-spoken, gentle, reliable, and patient, qualities that must have convinced both Mama and Keiko that he would make a devoted husband.

After the family moved to Los Angeles, I would look forward to their occasional visits. Keiko was very much like Papa. She had a way of making every night seem like a special celebration. She would tell humorous stories, do lively impersonations, and try out some of her newly rehearsed songs while Ted watched with amusement from the sidelines. They seemed like the ideal couple. Ultimately they separated. I never did find out what went wrong. I was still her kid sister, left in the dark, too young to be her confidant.

The escalator slowly rolled to the ground floor as I stood

scanning the airport for Keiko. I spotted her by the baggage carousel, dressed in a floral cotton gathered skirt, short-sleeved white blouse, and open-toed sling-backed heels. She looked much younger than her forty-two years, her short and loosely curled hair framing a heart-shaped face, smooth, translucent white skin, a dot for a nose, and large, dreamy eyes. She smiled when she saw me, revealing straight white teeth. Behind her stood a tall *haku-jin* (white) man, looking about the airport, acting like he was waiting for someone else, but I guessed from her description that he was her latest boyfriend, a thirty-two-year-old attorney whom she had met while working in the state building as a legal secretary. He was the first male companion after her divorce of six months past.

"My goodness! Is this my little sister?" she cried as I approached them with my purse, flight bag, and wardrobe case dangling from either shoulder. "Lewis, hurry! Help the poor girl," she ordered. He rushed forward to relieve me of the weight and stood peering sheepishly from behind his black horn rimmed glasses as she made the introductions.

"This is my baby sister, Akemi. She's going to be a doctor of anthropology—but not the kind that dig up bones."

"I heard a lot about you. Glad to make your acquaintance," he grinned.

Before an awkward moment could pass, Keiko instructed. "Well, get the car, Lewis. We'll wait for you out here."

He quickly exited through the automatic sliding glass doors and soon whipped his shiny white Pontiac around to a screeching stop at the sidewalk. He jumped out and neatly stacked my luggage into the trunk and I settled comfortably into the back seat.

Keiko chattered nonstop for the next twenty minutes until we reached her house. She leaned against the car door so she could get a better view of both of us as she talked. "You've got to tell me all about your trip. Lewis, did you know she went all the way to Japan to look up my mother's and father's relatives? Nobody from America has seen them before. She's writing a book about our family. Akemi, tell Lewis what you're doing."

Lewis sat stiffly behind the wheel, his eyes fixed to the road.

"I went to Japan to find out more about my parents' background," I answered obligingly. "Now I'm here to learn more about my sister and my family's early history."

"You see, Akemi's the youngest so we hardly know each other," Keiko explained. "I was married and out of the house before she was ten years old."

Lewis mechanically shook his head without uttering a word.

"There're eleven of us," she continued. Ten girls and one boy [two of my brothers had passed away when they were four years old]. I'm in the middle and she's the baby."

She glanced over at me from the corners of her eyes and tapped his arm: "Do you think we look alike?" Lewis turned around and the car bumped rapidly over the road dividers. "Hey! Watch where you're going," she barked. "You're going to get us killed."

We pulled into the driveway of Keiko's home, located in a quiet suburb of Sacramento. Her house was in a tract of identical homes built more than thirty years ago, but it distinctly stood out from the rest. The bright afternoon sun illuminated the freshly painted stucco walls and the neatly trimmed lawn looked greener than the parched brown grass of neighboring yards. Inside was just as immaculate as outside. The rooms were uncluttered, sensibly furnished in Sears Roebuck style. The table tops glistened, the windows sparkled, and the forest green shag rug was unmarked by footprints.

Lewis followed right behind us, setting my bags down in the living room. Then he headed straight for the kitchen, opened the refrigerator door and helped himself to a tall glass of orange juice. Flopping himself down on the naugahyde couch in the den and spreading his arms out wide, he wiggled all of his fingers, motioning Keiko to sit next to him.

"Lew-IS. You have to get back to the office," she whined.

"Not until I get my kiss," he insisted.

She pecked him quickly on the cheek and glanced over with embarrassment to see if I was watching. He wrapped his arms around her waist as she struggled to get back on her feet. "Let go. LET GO!" she screamed, hitting him over the head with a pillow. "Akemi's going to think you're a pervert."

"Aaaaghh!" he growled, trying to grab her again.

"Now be a good boy, Lewis, and go to work," she said, playfully messing up his soft ash-brown hair.

He reluctantly rose from the couch and went back to the refrigerator to pour himself another glass of juice. "What time is dinner tonight?" he asked between sips.

"Fend for yourself," she snapped. "We're going out to eat. And don't forget to drop off the tapes!" she shouted as he was halfway out of the door.

"But you won't be home."

"Then leave them on the front porch!" The door gently closed and she walked to the sink and promptly washed the juice glass.

"Is he always so obedient?" I asked.

"He just feels guilty because he doesn't spend enough time with me."

"How often does he come over?"

"Every night." She wiped her hands on a paper towel. "Are you tired?" Without waiting for an answer she continued. "Well, I told Hana we'd stop by to visit her today. We could take a leisurely ride to Liberty, stop and see all the places we used to live."

Hana, my second eldest sister, still lived in Liberty, the small grape-growing community where I grew up and had not revisited since we moved to Los Angeles twenty-one years ago. "Is the Paynes' house still there?" I asked excitedly, recalling the labor camp that Papa ran, the place where I had my fondest childhood memories.

"No. They tore that down long ago."

"What about the Mettlers' and the Smiths' houses?"

"They're gone too."

It was wishful thinking to assume those houses would still be standing. They were flimsy makeshift structures set back from the main roads and far away from the farm owners' dwellings. They were large enough to house our family and the transient laborers that Papa contracted each season to pick the grapes.

I sat in a lounge chair in Keiko's bedroom while she changed into bermuda shorts and a blue-and-white striped cotton tee-shirt. Proudly, she thrust her shoulders back, striking a pose in front of the mirror. "Not bad for an old broad, huh?" she asked, chuckling to herself. She still looked beautiful—a certain exuberance that I had never seen before set her face aglow.

We drove due south toward Liberty in the desiccating heat. The lush green vineyards stretched interminably, covering the flat valley floor with a heavy carpet of leaves. After twenty minutes of occasional farmhouses, clusters of trees and telephone poles rising like candles on a flat sheet of cake, Keiko made a sharp left turn onto a country road. "I think this is the way," she said, leaning forward, hugging the steering wheel. "See that store over there? That used to be 'Cooper's Corner.' The old man used to be a Jap hater. He'd wipe his hands on his pants every time we paid him, but he wanted our money so he'd take it—he was a merchant."

Another sudden turnoff to the side of the road found us parked in front of a schoolyard. She turned the engine off and we both sat in silence looking at a deserted playground through the curling waves of heat and the fine film of dust that settled gently on the hood of our car.

"See that swing?" she said in a hoarse whisper. "I would never swing on it because I was afraid that if I went too high, the children would catch a glimpse of my rice sack panties, see the big holes in my shoes." Her voice grew childlike, soft and milky. "I always ate there, away from the other kids." Keiko didn't want them to see what was inside her sandwich: a thin spread of mayonnaise barely reaching the edges. "I would quickly take it out of its wrapper and munch it down, pretending there was delicious meat inside."

Keiko and I both remembered the Langendorf bread wrapper Mama used to wrap our sandwiches in. It was waxy, thick, patterned like blue-and-white gingham, with a picture of a beautiful blue-eyed little girl in blond ringlets that cascaded to her shoulders. "I always wanted to be that girl," Keiko giggled softly.

"Well, anyway, I'd barely swallow my last bite and this girl Jane would come over and offer me her sandwich. I'd refuse because I didn't want her to think I was still hungry, or that we couldn't afford to have more in our lunches. Mom and Dad always said, 'Never take a bite from someone else's food.' Not only was it bad manners, but I had this feeling that it was dirty—just like kissing seemed so dirty. Besides, accepting food from Jane's hands took an act of courage! She was a snot eater. With one clean swoop she would use her forefinger to scrape the snot from her nose to her mouth."

"Ugh! That's the way I felt too, when I was young," I said, making a face.

"About snot eaters?" she asked.

"No. Kissing. It seemed so . . . unsanitary—passing spit from mouth to mouth!"

Keiko and I both laughed. "Yeah, only *haku-jin* people did that."

"The closest I ever came to seeing two Japanese people kiss was in the Japanese movies," I chuckled. Keiko smiled. At home, neither of us had ever seen Mama and Papa kiss—nor hug.

Keiko fixed her eyes on the weather-stained, wood-frame schoolhouse. "I hated school," she scowled. "All the inequities and insecurities would become tenfold. In the mornings we had to sing 'God Bless America,' and I would sit in the back of the class room and cry. How could that song mean anything to me? Christmas was the worst time of the year. The white girls always got to be the fairy princesses . . . 'Garlands of tinsel how brightly they gleam.' Nothing gleamed for me. One day I got to see inside this white boy's house. It had priscilla curtains, plush carpets, a bread box. Jane had a ball; Dick had a tricycle. How could I relate to this? We never saw a tricycle except in books. And the teacher would say, 'Read with expression, Kay.' But how could I? When we came home, Dad would reprimand us, 'Don't speak English!' I hated school. Our differences glared. At least at home I could live in my own fantasies, but when I got to school my dreams were shattered."

As I listened to Keiko recall her troubled past, I couldn't help but wonder whether her romance with Lewis was her way of gaining acceptance in a white world she could never be part of. Papa never would have dreamed that his harangueing would lead her into the arms of a *haku-jin*!

"Do you realize how difficult it is when your parents are telling you to be Japanese, be proud, don't try to look and act like a *haku-jin*, but yet because you are Japanese, you're not accepted at school?" Keiko asked, not waiting for an answer. "You could feel the distinct racism. You know you're not considered equal. I remember when we went to school in Arkansas we'd play games during recess and the kids always made us be the babies because we were small. They thought of us as little China dolls from under the sea, from the other side of the world, lichee nuts, silk . . . we were novelty items, little trinkets, little toys. They didn't know the racism that Californians knew—to hate, to fear, to be suspicious of us because we had weird, mysterious ways."

Asians were never a problem in Arkansas. There were never enough of us. But the blacks in Arkansas were familiar with the kind of racism directed at the Japanese in California. Both strains of prejudice had a long time to fester over the decades, to become accepted as a way of life, an integral part of family and social histories, and to become institutionalized into the legal fabric of state and local governments. I knew what Keiko meant when she said, "You could feel the distinct racism." Every adult who had experienced the camps, every child who grew up with its specter, was familiar with the taste, look, and feel of society's contempt, fear, and distrust of people of Japanese ancestry. We might have left Arkansas far behind us, but the stigma of the camps continued to intrude upon our lives, especially after we started public school.

Sharing the bitter childhood memories seemed to ease some of the pain and slowly the deep furrows between Keiko's brows began to relax, her face growing serenely calm. She silently looked at the schoolyard, fixing the image in her mind for the last time before starting the engine.

"I'll take you to the Paynes' but you won't recognize it," she warned. My heart beat rapidly, afraid to face the drastic changes that twenty-one years of absence could bring. "It's just up ahead," she pointed. "Right where that tree stands."

"No! It can't be," I insisted. "There were *two* large trees much bigger than that one." I distinctly remembered those oak trees that stood side by side like two watchful giants towering over the labor camp, branches spreading over the mess hall, shading the sleeping quarters, the shower room, and the bathhouse. Their leaves would cast fantasy shadows: by day, a rippling stretch of dappled sunlight forming make-believe rivulets and islands; by night, a sea of purple waves tinted by moonlight, dancing with the gentle sway of the valley breeze.

"Where's the walnut tree?" I persisted. It used to stand by itself, next to the mess hall, dwarfed by the size of the impressive oaks. Papa had made a swing for that tree and under its branches the workmen gathered after dinner, telling us stories about Japan, adventures in Hawaii, their experiences in America.

"And what about all the buildings?" I asked. I was thinking particularly of the mess hall because that's where the family spent the most time together, cooking, eating, singing, talking. I could distinctly remember Papa cooking sardines in the mess hall, the smoke so thick that I felt I had walked into a cloud bank when I entered the room. There he stood before the stove, singing as he fried the fish he had caught that morning. Papa's eyes glistened. He loved every aspect of fishing—catching it, cooking it, and eating it—and he had honed each step into a fine art. As he skillfully turned each sardine over to brown, he must have been thinking of how delicious they would taste with the hot, simmering rice.

"I know this is the right place, Akemi," Keiko insisted. "You just remember everything being big because you were so little." We turned down a narrow dirt road plowed between the vineyards. "I think this is the way to the river," she continued, pressing her face closer toward the windshield.

When we reached the end of the road, I quickly got out of the car, lost in my excitement to see the place I loved so dearly. The river always held mysterious secrets for me. A workman had hanged himself from one of the trees along the banks; another had drowned in a whirlpool. And once before dusk I swore I saw from a distance the floating ghostlike figure of a headless man on a white horse prancing along the river's edge. It was a place forbidden, majestic, eerie, sacred, its shores once the home of the Chulamni Indians whose spirits still lingered.

Mama and Papa would never let me walk down to the river alone so I would go with my sister Hiromi (ninth eldest daughter), and together, clutching hands, we would walk the river's banks, daring the smooth white sand that slipped between our toes to suck us into the dark rushing water. "Never swim here," we were warned. "The currents are too swift." So Hiromi and I would venture no further, admiring the water's beauty from a measured distance.

I shrank back from the sight before me. The years of drought had sapped the river of its strength, its main body withered, the tributaries parched, the foliage sparse. I turned around to see if Keiko shared my disappointment, but I found her still standing by the car, gazing in the opposite direction.

As I approached she spoke barely above a whisper. "I didn't think I'd ever want to see another vine as long as I lived. I worked too long in the fields with Mom, Dad, Chieko, Hana, and Kenji. I picked grapes from the moment I got out of grammar school . . . all summer long." I looked at her frail body stunted by the size of the sprawling vine, and found it hard to imagine how she could have sustained such grueling work.

August marked the beginning of the grape season and that was when the Paynes' camp came alive. My brother Kenji would drive the big truck into Los Angeles and try to persuade workers to come to our camp. "We have better meals, larger crops," he would say, and after a week or two he would come back with thirty to fifty men. Some men were recruited locally and others were regulars who found their way back year after year.

Half of the men were Kibei, born in the United States and educated in Japan; the other half were Issei, born in Japan. The work crews that Kenji and Papa recruited were usually quite fast. Some of the men used to pack 150 to 160 boxes a day, whereas

Keiko would manage about 70.

The workers got paid according to their output and a mixture of pride and competition infused their work. Who works the fastest and cleanest was always the topic of each season. The picker would bring his boxes to the aisle and our brother Kenji would come along, inspect them, and nail the lids on; then the swamper would load them onto the truck. Since Papa was the foreman and contractor, he would go around and examine the boxes to see that they were neatly packed. Papa made sure to place the best picker's boxes on the top of the shipment since those were the ones that were usually checked for quality cleanliness, weight, and sugar content. If it didn't pass inspection, the fruit would be kicked back and nobody got paid. Since Papa received a percentage for each box picked, the family would hold their breath and pray.

One summer Kenji managed to recruit about five young Nisei, second generation American-born Japanese, who were looking for jobs during their summer break from college. I remember all the excitement they created the night they arrived.

My brother rolled in that evening at about eight with thirty men, the first arrivals for the season. He led them into the bottom floor of the sleeping barracks where beds were lined up, army style. A mad scramble ensued as the men dashed to secure the best spots, the beds in the corners of the room or by the windows.

One of the men peered through a hole in the wall that looked into the family's sleeping quarters and shouted gleefully, "OOOooohh-WEEEEeeee! There're some girls next door!" I guess Kenji had never told them about all his sisters.

Midori (seventh eldest daughter) quickly grabbed the mosquito repellent and sprayed a shot through the hole: "That'll teach 'em," she said, holding the dispenser like a machine gun ready to assault the next peeping tom. We all giggled and waited for the victim who would follow. We could hear the men pushing and shoving, jockeying to get into the right position. As another eye bobbed into view Midori expertly squirted another shot into the hole.

"Aagh! She got me!" yelled one victim.

"Hey! Move over," whooped another, aroused by the challenge.

The noise quieted down when Kenji entered their quarters. "Eh, follow me. I'll show you where the *benjo* [toilets] and the showers are."

Midori got a piece of cardboard and tacked it up over the hole and for the rest of the night we could hear the men talking, unpacking their bags, and settling into the small spaces that they would call home for the next several months.

The following morning they awoke and found a kitchen full of young women serving them breakfast before they trudged off to the fields. Keiko was seventeen, still a senior in high school; Yoko, fifteen; Midori, fourteen; Harumi, thirteen; Hiromi, nine, and I was seven.

During summer vacations, the three eldest sisters and Kenji had to work in the fields with Mama and Papa and the workmen. Harumi, Hiromi, and I got to stay at home to tend to household chores which we quickly finished off in the morning. The rest of the day was spent playing, but Harumi never joined us. She felt she was too old for our childish games. And when Hiromi turned ten, she also began to feel that she was too mature to play with me.

But as dusk approached, we were thrust together again because she and I had to collect grape logs and start the fire for the Japanese bath as Harumi prepared the rice. Soon Mama and the older sisters would return from the fields to start the evening meal while Papa, Kenji, and the workmen showered or bathed and rested before dinner.

The bath was an evening ritual that Papa thoroughly enjoyed and consequently the *o-furo-ba* (bathhouse) was one of the first structures erected wherever we moved. The bath was used for soaking and relaxation, never for cleansing oneself. A thorough scrub with soap and water before entering the bath ensured that the water remained clean for the next bather.

At times I had to bathe with Papa, something I thoroughly dreaded because in the bathing hierarchy, Papa always bathed first, when the water was the cleanest and by far the hottest. No matter how scalding hot the water, it never seemed to faze Papa. He liked his bath water bubbling hot, just like his soup. He probably needed the deep heat to penetrate his aching muscles and melt away the pain. But I always felt certain that I was being boiled alive, my body a crimson ball of steam by the time Papa felt I was ready to be plucked out of the water. The bath felt good only after I got out and the cool air restored my light-headedness and body temperature back to normal.

The best part of the evening was after everyone ate and the sisters sang while doing the dishes. The workmen would gather under the walnut tree to listen appreciatively. "You girls sound better than the Andrews sisters," they would compliment. And the requests would follow: "Tennessee Waltz," "Harbor Lights," "Detour." The repertoire was endless.

Several of the workmen were talented musicians. Osamu played the *shakuhachi* (a five-holed bamboo flute), Johnny the harmonica, and Wada the mandolin, their instruments providing the only stability in their transient existence. Each night Wada lovingly polished his mandolin, handling it like a delicate young maiden, his long, willowy fingers gingerly slipping the flannel cloth between the frets, along the neck, over the soundboard and coming to rest on the bridge. After completing this evening ritual, he would lean back against the porch railing and play the mandolin, watching Keiko through the screen door as she moved about in the kitchen. A faint smile would creep over his lips, pleased by the mastery he had achieved with his instrument and excited by the effect that his music seemed to have upon her. Keiko loved the plaintive sounds of his mandolin, particularly when he played the Japanese songs that she knew by heart.

All the men found Keiko enchanting but none was as persistent or daring as Wada in trying to capture her attention. He fought to work next to her in the fields, carrying her boxes if she fell behind. He paraded around in brief swimming trunks in the bitter cold of winter just to impress her with his physique. But the harder he tried to win her, the more she ignored him. His pursuit was futile from the start, for even if she took a fancy to him, Papa would have never allowed any of the itinerant workers to marry his daughters.

Each new season brought a crop of admiring workmen like Wada and an abundance of secret stories shared only by the elders. And by October, when the last man left with the season's end, only the stories remained to breathe life into the deserted labor camp. It was a lonely time of year, a long winter to survive until the following harvest.

For Mama and Papa, the years at the Paynes' Camp foreshadowed a turning point in their lives, the end of contract farming. After Kenji left home to go to school in Los Angeles, Papa realized that he could not manage the work without his son's help and decided to move into the town of Liberty. I'm not quite sure what his plans were when we moved from the Paynes', but he probably wasn't thinking too far beyond the immediate reality of not being able to manage by himself. Mama said he was tired, fed up with farm work. His back seemed to ache more each year. And knowing there weren't too many good years left where he could work as hard as he did, he probably questioned from time to time whether he could really rely on his son to take care of him and Mama in old age.

I am sure that Papa, being as proud as he was, would not have accepted old age very graciously, especially if he had to depend on his children for financial support. But he didn't have many options. Farming was the only kind of work he could secure, and although he continued to gamble, I think that by then he had come to realize he wasn't going to make that "big score." His bankroll was never substantial enough to be part of such a game. I suppose his only ace in the hole was Kenji, and now that Kenji was leaving for Los Angeles the assurance that he would fulfill the duties and obligations he owed to his parents was in jeopardy.

We lived at the Paynes' for only three years, but it seemed much longer to me. I had spent almost half of my childhood there. I was eight years old when we moved, and I cried hopelessly when the truck carrying our belongings pulled out of the dirt driveway for the last time, leaving all my secret hiding places behind. For me the camp had meant freedom, a boundless playground for exploration, and I felt that I would never find another place more dear. But as for my elder sisters, they probably looked forward to the faster-paced excitement of town.

Mama must have been overjoyed too. We were moving to a newly built house. Already the sisters had planned the color scheme for each room and had sewn curtains to match. The only foreboding she may have felt was that we now lived closer to the gambling dens. But being the optimist that she was, she felt that the town would open up new avenues for her to make money, and besides, at last she was going to live in a real house, the first one she lived in since coming to America.

I know that for Keiko the years at the Paynes' were remembered with anguish, as a time fraught with conflicting emotions—hating school but finding no refuge at home, of knowing she was different and longing to be like everyone else, of craving love and attention yet feeling guilty about the growing sexuality welling inside.

While Keiko was laboring in the fields alongside the men, picking grapes, and transforming the workmen into her favorite matinee idols, I stayed at home listening to "Lorenzo Jones," playing with paper dolls, and dreaming about the day I could fly without wings.

Now twenty-one years later, as Keiko and I stood quietly by the the roadside, I could hear the faint sounds of our brother nailing the lids on the boxes, of Papa singing songs from the old country to lighten the day's work, of the shears clipping the juicy, red bunches of Tokays, and I could imagine Mama and her daughters working as fast and efficiently as Joe and Tony, two of Papa's fastest workers. In our silence I realized that the ten years between us had finally closed its gap. We were both women.

As Keiko and I traveled away from the river back to the main road, I looked over at the brick house where Mr. and Mrs. Payne used to live. The house looked much smaller and less cared for than the elegant structure I remembered. The prize-winning rose bushes that Mrs. Payne treasured so dearly no longer graced their front yard. Instead, a healthy patch of weeds took their place and threatened to dominate the rest of the garden.

"Look, is that Mr. Payne?" I asked, pointing to an outline of a tall, shadowy figure that stood watching our car from behind a large bay window.

"Probably," Keiko answered. We had both spotted their name on the mailbox at the side of the road before driving down to the river.

"Should we stop and say hello?" I asked, kind of curious to see the man whose name was all I remembered about him.

"What for?" Keiko answered matter-of-factly. She had no intention of stopping. I'm sure Mr. Payne would have remembered us. Papa worked for him for over three years. He was also the one to identify Papa's body when they dredged it up from the river. But those years probably left a deeper impression in our lives than they did in Mr. Payne's. We were just another family that had come to work for him.

Keiko made a sharp right turn on to the country road and headed east for the town of Liberty. "That's the last time I'll see that place again," she said, heaving a sigh of relief. She didn't bother to look back although I watched until the house dropped out of sight, enveloped by the sea of sprawling vineyards.

5

The Elder Sisters

*W*e pulled into a long gravel driveway and were immediately accosted by a big German shepherd running alongside our car, barking ferociously each step of the way. When we came to a stop, she planted herself at the front of the car, growling, baring her canines and daring us to get out.

"Reba! Down girl!" Hana shouted from the top of her back porch steps. "Don't be afraid of her. She's just a harmless ol' grouch—she won't bite."

"Can't convince me, Hana. Look at all that saliva running down her mouth," said Keiko, electing to remain in the car.

"I tell you, she's harmless." Hana held her tightly by the collar and bent over to peer into the car. "Harumi? Yoko? Ah, Akemi. Of course, it's you." Hana broke into a warm smile. She hadn't seen me since her last visit to Los Angeles over seven years before. "Come inside. Nesan's here. We've been waitin' for you guys all morning."

In my adulthood I had never spent much time with my two eldest sisters. The occasional family gatherings were what brought us together very briefly over the years. Nesan was twenty years older than I, Hana nineteen. Both were married in Rohwer, Arkansas, the concentration camp where I was born.

Nesan's eldest child, Jeanette, was only one month younger than I, but she acted like she was much older, always managing to set the tone and dominate the play activities on her weekly visits to our house. Much of her dominance over me had to do with her physical size. She was stocky and solid whereas I was wiry and lean, our physical constitutions mirrored our diets. She was raised on meat, milk, and butter while I was used to fish, vegetables, and rice. Our birth order in our families also affected how we related to each other. Jeanette was the eldest in a family of three girls and two boys and was used to giving orders and having her way, whereas I was the youngest of eleven, at the end of the assembly line where all orders stopped. Nobody had to obey my commands.

I felt much more comfortable with Hana's son Peter. He was quiet and shy, much like me, and together few words were exchanged in our active games of make-believe. Sometimes his younger sister Irene tagged along, but she had a hard time keeping up with us as we ran through cornfields, jumped irrigation ditches, and scrambled up and down castles built out of grape boxes.

I could still remember the gleam in Peter's eyes as he decided to prepare the goldfish for a *sashimi* (raw fish) lunch. He had often watched his mother do the same with the striped bass that his father had caught in the San Joaquin River. The goldfish desperately fought for his life, twisting and leaping off the cutting board as Peter tried to attack his gills. Peter did manage to shave off a few scales before returning him safely to his bowl and settling for a bologna sandwich instead.

If Hana or Nesan had any problems in their personal lives, I would have been one of the last persons in the family to whom they would have divulged their secrets. To them, I was their children's playmate. To me, they were of another generation, each old enough to be my mother.

Hana had prepared the perfect lunch for a hot summer's day: cold buckwheat noodles with a mushroom-fish broth, sprinkled with green onions and seaweed, and topped off with sliced hard-boiled eggs. After eating, we all settled in the living room. It was a chance for them to reminisce, and an opportunity for me to learn more about the family's early history.

Keiko headed straight for the couch. "Oooh . . . I'm so-o-oh tired," she complained, draping her frail body over the cushions.

"Keiko. You look absolutely terrible!" remarked Hana. Only a sister could get away with making such a comment without raising Keiko's ire.

"She was always sickly as a child," I reminded Hana. Keiko was looking for sympathy, not criticism.

Keiko cast a mischievous smile. "That was mostly an act. But do you remember when I had an ovarian cyst removed when I was only nineteen? Well, that time I was really sick and I was in my glory because Mom was fussing over me."

"I was always playin' sick too," Hana laughed. "It didn't work though—Mama was too smart. There were times when Nesan [eldest daughter] or Naomi [third eldest daughter] was ill and I wanted to get sick so bad that I'd watch where they drank from a cup, and when they put it down, I'd measure and drink from the exact spot, just to get sick! But I never did. *Baka* [dumb], huh?"

Getting special, individual attention from Mama was difficult in a family as large as ours. That's why sickness played a significant part in our lives because it was the only time when we got Mama's undivided attention. She would prepare special foods, usually soft rice, sour plums, and jello, and would hover over us until we got well. On those occasions, even Papa would get a little jealous. "Come to bed!" he'd tell her. "You're at your best when the children are sick." But Mama had lost two children to sickness and she wasn't taking any chances of losing another.

"Nesan, do you remember the couple that wanted you so bad?" asked Hana.

"Which couple?"

"You know. The one in L. A."

"I don't remember them well," Nesan answered, preferring not to talk about them.

"I slept over there once and when I woke up—BOY! Did I give that woman a bad time," Hana recalled. "I knew that woman wanted you and I thought Daddy left me there in exchange for you."

"I remember that," Keiko interjected, although she was not even born at the time. "The woman told Mom, 'You're so young that you could have more children. Please! Let me have her! What's minus one? You could still have a slug of others!'" Keiko turned to me to fill me in on more of the details. Clearly, she had heard this story many times before. "You see, Mom already had four kids at the time and the lady was sterile. Mom felt so bad that one night, without warning, they packed their bags and fled. Did you know that, Nesan?"

"No. That I didn't know," Nesan flatly replied, seemingly uninterested in the story.

Keiko continued. "They left L. A. because that lady harped and harped about having you. And she was so nice to Mom. She sewed clothes for you, broke her neck to talk Mom into—"

"Oh, I can't get over Nesan," Hana interrupted. "I can't get over her! She blocked everything out that she don't want to remember—"

"I have a bad memory," Nesan insisted, fidgeting in her chair, obviously annoyed.

"Do you remember the place we lived before Kettleman's?" Hana persisted.

"I don't," Nesan answered curtly, refusing to get caught up in their game of "memory lane."

"Ha!" Keiko mocked in disbelief.

"I really don't!"

Hana proceeded to describe vague images in an attempt to refresh her memory. "There was lotsa shade. I see big trees . . . I remember pickin' up acorns—"

"Wasn't that the shack next to Shimono's?" Keiko guessed.

"No," Hana answered confidently. "I know that house. I used to jump from the roof. But this place—it was long and gloomy—"

"It was Shimono's!" Keiko insisted.

"No, it wasn't. I remember everything about Shimono's!"

"Then tell me about the middle room," Keiko challenged.

"That was where you kids slept, and—"

"What was on the walls!"

"Well, *that* I can't remember," Hana conceded.

Keiko finally stumped her and she smiled triumphantly. "It was plastered with newspaper. And you guys would play games. You'd lie on the bed and say, 'Okay, which one?' And we were supposed to guess which word you found. And do you remember the first bedroom? There was a big King snake under the bed—came right through the floor boards—"

"And the screen door don't fit too good," Hana continued in the same breath. "In the mornings here come this chicken. It was her daily ritual, layin' eggs. She come in there and sit down and I'd get down low and watch her drop her egg. And just when the egg is ready to come out, she stands and squats her bottom down: Uuuu-mppphhhhh! She's pushin'! She's really workin' at it. Pretty quick her bottom starts spreadin' open and, Pu-u-u-rrrt, Po-TON! Out comes a real soft egg. Then she'll sit on it."

Hana had us all laughing as she went through the egg-laying motions of the chicken. Then the laughter settled to silence before Hana chose to talk again.

"All my life . . . I didn't have confidence. You see, there was Nesan above me and Naomi below. Both weren't ordinary—they were exceptionally bright. And they were pretty on top of it. These Issei people would come over and keep talkin' about you. Do you remember, Nesan?"

"No."

" 'Aah! What a beauty!' they'd say. Do you remember that? We must have been about fourteen, fifteen and you and me, we were eatin' at the Chop Suey restaurant and this old man, Ouchi, the *bakatare* [dummy]! He was sittin' at another table just dro-o-o-lin' and dotin' on your good looks, mumblin', 'Ah, how beautiful, how *BEAU-TI-FUL!*' And I'm hurt. I'm thinkin' to myself, 'You sour fool. How crude!' And I guess he noticed the lost look on my face and he says, 'Oh, you're pretty too.' I was so embarrassed—I could've clubbed him one—he made it worse."

"But, but Hana," Nesan stuttered. "*YOU* were the pretty one—not me. You acted so, so confident—"

"What?" Hana asked in disbelief. "Now what makes you think that! You got the word from people all your life! Even Mama used to say, 'Nesan is a *beppin-san* [beauty].' And she always said that about Chieko [fourth eldest daughter] too—"

"But you always acted so, so—"

"Conceited?" Hana relieved Nesan of the word she did not want to say. "It was just a front. I used to think to myself: 'I'm goin' to be pretty when I grow up. I'm goin' to be pretty. *I'M GOIN' TO BE PRETTY!* Someday I'll show them that I'm pretty too!'"

"Hana, I would have never guessed," Keiko gasped with disbelief. "You were always so vain, concerned about your appearance—"

"I told Mama one day. 'Why is it that you gave me such a bad lookin' face, and on top of that, I've got your nose, Mama—I ain't got no nose!' And she says to me, 'Hana-chan, you won't look good with a nose any different from the one you got. But if it bothers you so much, pinch your bridge like this, and it'll get taller.' So every night—it was a ritual—I'd squeeze it to bring it up. See?" Hana demonstrated the procedure. "It worked! It used to be flat and wide, just a button on there—like Mama's."

Keiko started to laugh uncontrollably. I'm sure that she had practiced the same ritual but the results were not the same. "Well, no one could have had a bigger complex about their nose than I," she said self-consciously. "Kenji and you guys used to tease me constantly about this ugly, flat nose. Kenji used to call me 'Pipe Nose,' straight and ugly with two holes at the end. He called Nesan 'Mushroom Nose.' But no one else had a nose quite like mine. To this day, I don't like anybody looking at it very long because I'm convinced it looks like a pipe."

Hana glanced sheepishly at Keiko. "Did I used to call you that too?"

"Oh, yes! And you used to say that I was dark complected and that I talked too much—"

"Oh yeah. Now that you mention it," Hana grinned. "Your mouth never shut up and you'd out-talk me—"

"MOTOR MOUTH!" Keiko shouted.

"Was I the only one that was mean to you like that?"

"No. All the older ones were."

"Well, that's the way it was in our family," Hana explained. "The younger ones had to obey the older ones."

"But you only had Nesan to contend with," retorted Keiko.

"But Nesan was powerful." Hana released a nervous laugh. "Nesan, you really were." Nesan sat silently, her eyes cast downward. "Yes, you used to boss everyone around, even Mom. But Dad never bawled you out for it. I used to resent it."

"I was always making someone cry," Nesan said apologetically. "I know."

"Nesan was so *kishomen na* [neat]," Keiko added, trying to ease Nesan's discomfort. "And us little kids would dirty the house right after she'd clean up so she'd make us stay outside all day. Only time we got to come inside was for the meals and to go to sleep."

Hana chuckled. "She'd get the washboard and scrub all them sheets. And as I got older, I'd act like I had a backache so I didn't have to help her."

"I used to weed all the yard, clean the house—all that really bothered me," Nesan interjected, trying to justify her behavior.

"Oh, I used to be so scared of you, Nesan," Keiko quavered.

Hana chimed right in. "She was powerful and she was spoiled. I knew that she was Daddy's only daughter. I hated her—she was bossy, and she was Daddy's favorite." Hana smiled. Her eyes twinkled. She was pleased that she could tell Nesan all the feelings she had harbored for more than forty years. "Papa was a hard man to please. I thought if I was like a boy, he would care for me a little bit more. I did my best to act tomboyish. Nesan, you were good at crocheting, doin' things in the house. Me, I thought I'd get on Dad's good side by workin' in the fields. I'd compete with the workmen, and everything they did, I'd do just as good. But as far as I'm concerned, I just didn't exist for Daddy."

"Now, Hana." Keiko protested, sitting up straight to make her point. "You were always one of Daddy's favorites!"

"No!" Hana answered adamently. "Dad just had Nesan. She was the only one until Kenji came along, then Dad had a kid again. Isn't that right Nesan?"

"Well, I think I was Daddy's—"

"See! She knows it. See! SHE KNOWS IT ALL!" Hana excitedly jumped up from her chair, exultant that after all of these years she had finally extracted an unspoken fact out of her older sister.

"I don't remember Nesan all too well," said Keiko. "But Chieko [fourth eldest daughter], she was the apple of Dad's eye."

"That I didn't know," Nesan commented.

"I knew that," Hana quickly offered. "Nesan, Kenji, and Chieko were the three kids he had. The rest were *hanakuso* [snot]! Dad had two sets of eyes. If you was his favorite, he never saw anything wrong, but if it was me, he'd see it in one minute. He'd needle me. Pick on me. I couldn't do anything right!"

"Poor Yoko [sixth eldest daughter]," Keiko lamented. "I remember him tormenting her because she was so headstrong and he wanted to make us girls obedient—"

"Actually, the only big coward was me," Hana interjected. "All my life, all I could think about was pleasin' him. If he told me to crawl, I'd crawl all day long if I thought that's what it'll take to make him happy."

"But Daddy had his good qualities too," Nesan said defensively, her face now fully revealing the irritation she tried to hide.

"Oh yes!" Hana was quick to agree. "Daddy was a man who never made us feel like we were poor. If he had money, he was goin' to have his kids live! Take us to a movie—make a game out of everything. I tell you, he was a very exciting man—"

"And proud too!" Nesan reminded Hana.

"Yes, yes, yes!" Hana replied, hammering her fists on the arms of the chair. "He wasn't goin' to take any crap from no one. I remember once Daddy took us to buy shoes at J. C. Penney's. There was two or three of us kids and we lined up and sat there. The salesman was actin' like, 'Here come some Jap kids. I guess I have to wait on 'em.' I was a kid but I sensed it and I was kinda hurt by it. Well, you know how Dad is. He says to the guy, 'You tired? If you're tired, I don't want you waitin' on us. I want to see the manager!' My, the guy suddenly perked up and gave us the best service. Dad came laughin' home. 'Boy, I put that guy straight,' he says. 'He gave us service, didn't he?' And you know the shoes he bought for me? They were the cheapest ones in the store—a give-away. They were the kind that bar girls in Western movies wore with tights—high heeled shoes laced up to the thigh. I yanked the heels off and ruined 'em pretty quick so I didn't have to wear 'em."

"And do you remember what a big to-do he made about his appearance?" Keiko remarked. "He had to have a crease down his pants, starched collar, and a clean white hankie." She jumped up from the couch, mimicking Papa, and for the first time since the conversation began, Nesan smiled. "Remember the royal blue suit he bought for Naomi's wedding?" asked Keiko. "Well, he felt like a million bucks! He was sure he looked like Humphrey Bogart, better than Errol Flynn, and more masculine than—who's that other guy I'm trying to think of—"

"RANDOLPH SCOTT," Hana answered.

"That's right. He fancied he looked like them. He knew he was good looking—he didn't mince words about it. I think Mom was proud of him. I was proud of him—when he was dressed up—because I knew nobody else's father looked as good as our Dad . . . but I was ashamed of Mom. Poor Mom . . . she always looked so shabby. I was ashamed of her because she didn't look like the other mothers. I was ashamed of her because she was pregnant. I was ashamed of her because she acted so humble. I was ashamed of her because she couldn't speak English."

The room suddenly fell silent, only the sound of passing cars could be heard from the highway. Keiko's confession had struck a sensitive core in all of us. I know it had for me. There were times, when I was much younger, that Mama's foreignness filled me with embarrassment. This secret that I harbored within, brought me much guilt, for as a child I loved my mother more than anyone else in the world. Although I knew that her tenderness could melt glaciers and her fearlessness could frighten even the most spiteful gods, she still looked and acted foreign to others.

My mother did not glide through crowded rooms in high-heeled shoes, but instead, she wore leather work boots that were more practical for laboring in the fields. My mother did not wear bright red nail polish, full gathered skirts, and flowering hats, but instead she donned homemade bonnets that shaded her face from the hot northern California sun, and she wore loose fitting trousers that would give her room to bend as she harvested the seasonal crops. And she kept her nails cut short, to the quick, so that the itchy red peat dirt of the Sacramento Delta would not have a chance to cling to her already chafed skin.

Despite the times when I had witnessed her courage and determination, the stronger emotion I felt inside of me was embarrassment. I clearly remembered one hot summer vacation when I was about eight years old; Mama tightly held my hand as we walked ten miles in the 105 degree sun to buy me a new pair of shoes. She had just had a blistering argument with Papa because he had gambled away the family's summer savings. I don't know where she found the extra cash to buy me those shoes—probably in one of the tin cans that she had buried around the yard to keep them hidden from Papa—but she was determined that I would not return to school with holes in my shoes.

I will never forget those new shoes. They were impractical, shiny, black patent leather, the kind that little girls wore on Easter Sunday—not at all like the ones that I usually got with tractor-tire soles that lasted me for a whole year.

Mama gingerly peeled out each dollar bill to pay the salesperson, the money crumpled, sweat-stained, precious, but she was determined to save me from the ridicule of mocking children. And though I knew that in my heart, all I could think about at the time was "I hope none of my friends see me with my mother."

Hana was the first to interrupt the stillness in the room. "The fighting. That's what I'll never forget. I always sided for Dad because I was scared of 'im. But you, Nesan. Being the oldest you could've stuck up for Mom, but instead you sided for Dad—"

"Because Mom was such a weakling to me," Nesan answered defensively. "I felt Mama didn't have . . . I wanted to see—"

"More backbone," Hana finished Nesan's sentence. "Well, the reason why I sided for Dad was because—"

"There was no percentage—" Keiko interrupted.

"I didn't want to be on his bad side.," Hana continued. "Mom was goin' to be good to me anyway. There was no reason for me to try to please or butter her up 'cause I knew she really loved me."

Nesan sat quietly in the chair, her hands tightly gripping the arms, tears slowly welling in her eyes. "I really wasn't much comfort to mother . . . I really wasn't . . . ."

"Nesan, you needn't feel guilty," Hana said, trying to comfort her. "We all felt that way. Now we say, 'Mama, Mama, Mama,' because we are old enough to see things . . ."

Nesan kept shaking her head. "After I started having children, I really realized that I wasn't fair to Mama . . . what she had to tolerate just for us . . ."

Keiko stood up and walked to the bay window, gazing solemnly out at the laden vines now ready for harvest. "After you guys started having children, you'd talk about Mom, how good, how sweet. But I couldn't understand what you were taking about. I had no respect for her because she was still letting Dad mow her down! I wanted her to stick up for herself, tell Dad off, fight back!"

"But that was Mom's only weakness," Hana reasoned. "Otherwise, she was such a powerful woman, but when it came to Dad . . ."

Keiko nodded her head in agreement. "We just didn't realize the bullshit she put up with, just for us. If she hadn't, our family would be scattered away." She turned to look at each of us, her eyes looking for forgiveness. "You know, up to the year Dad died, I was still telling her to leave him. I couldn't understand why she couldn't take him by the horns and shake him loose!"

"Me too," Hana admitted. "I'd tell her, 'For the life of me! I can't understand any woman stayin' with a man like that. If I was you, Mama, I'd get rid of 'im. Chuck 'im. I'll take care of you!' Huh! Idiot me. I was just a teenager. How could she rely on me. But I couldn't stand the fightin'."

Nesan sat quietly removed from the rest of us, her eyes brimming with tears, her lips tightly pursed. She would never have told Mama to leave Papa. She did not believe in divorce.

Her tears spoke for our shame that we all felt inside. Only after we became mothers and wives did we begin to appreciate and understand the struggles that Mama had to endure. We had misunderstood her humility and perseverance as signs of weakness; we had discovered that it was much more difficult to weather a bad marriage for the sake of the children rather than to follow our own personal desires and goals.

Keiko's voice trembled as she searched our faces for answers. "Why was he so angry? Why did he treat Mom like that? We'd yell at her, 'Stop talking back to him! Don't say anything more! Just let him rant and rave!' Because when she talked back, tried to reason with him, or verbally defend herself, he'd get violently angry. He wants to gamble. He wants to use our life savings, our grocery money. He wants to spend the money that Mom wants to send back to Japan. And time and time again, he'd go humiliating her in front of others. He'd be sitting there at the mess table and I don't know what the hell he's angry about, but Mama would bring him a dish, then he'd knock it away and the dish and food would go scurrying all over the table to the floor. He didn't like the way she brought the dish over to him; he didn't like the way it was prepared; Mom didn't put her heart into it; the rice wasn't cooked properly. Then after the outburst, he'd say, 'I'm going!' And he'd go stomping out to town, to the gambling house. Mom, she cried a lot . . . but mostly she'd be brave. She would take it. And later she'd laugh about the incident. I'd think to myself, 'Mom, how could you laugh after we were so scared for you? How could you laugh when we were so sad? How could you humor Dad after that? How could you even touch him? Oh! I couldn't understand! Then at night he'd come home after gambling, singing and trying to humor us. How were we supposed to take it? Huh? And each night he would build parables around incidents that happened throughout the day. Each had a moral. He'd teach us things of beauty, truth, lessons that not even Jesus preached about. Yet the same day he'd carry on like that with Mom. I know I have the fortitude that others don't have because of Dad's teachings. But, oh! The fear, the conflict, the anxiety he left in my mind will never be erased!"

A deathly stillness filled the room. It was Papa. He could still evoke tears, anger, and laughter. He still played an active part in our lives, held a tenacious grip on our minds even twenty-one years after his death.

Papa's influence left a deep imprint on everybody's life, but the only one who continued to live up to the ideals that he so often preached about was Nesan. Widowed at age thirty (her husband and father-in-law died in the same boating accident along with my father), she never remarried, raising her five children and taking care of her mother-in-law until the latter's death some twenty years later. She was a mirror-image of Mama—dutiful, self-sacrificing, strong-willed, and determined to see her children through college at all costs. In her life, the children came first, before personal ambition, dreams, or desires. She was a rare breed, a Meiji woman like Mama. We all admired and respected her for her selflessness and strength.

Nesan held a special place in the family order. She was ne-san, elder sister, the firstborn, and with that role she assumed the greatest responsibility of all. She had to be the role model to her nine younger sisters. Mama and Papa knew they could depend on her. She was exceptionally bright, perceptive, filial, and mature beyond her years. And because they were not thoroughly schooled in American ways and the English language, and were barred from holding the legal status of an American citizen, they found themselves relying on her even more, turning to her for assistance and advice.

The problems and worries that came to rest upon her shoulders at such an early age had deprived Nesan of a carefree youth and set her even further apart from the rest of us. She lived in a separate world, acted on a different plane, one that was closer to Mama's and Papa's. No sibling challenged her authority; nobody was her equal. In fact, according to Hana, who is only one year younger than Nesan, that afternoon was the first time that both Hana and Keiko were able to pry into Nesan's past. She could have revealed more about the family history than anyone else, but she refused to talk about the past. She claimed that she could not remember, but I had the suspicion that even if she could, she was not going to divulge her memories. They were private thoughts, not meant to be shared with us or even with her own children.

I have often wondered. Why the reticence? Is it because she truly cannot remember? Was the past so painful that she had banished it from her memory? Or was it the same *shikata ga nai* (it can't be helped), let bygones-be-bygones attitude that helped to silence the concentration-camp experience from our conversations with our children? Whatever the reason, I was not going to press her. Nesan had her right to silence.

As we sat quietly lost in our thoughts, the ambivalence that I had always held toward Papa slowly resurfaced. I admired him because he made us feel proud we were Japanese, but I hated him for treating Mama so poorly, for making her life so miserable. I felt both fortunate and deprived that he had passed away when I was only nine. I was glad, as I listened to my sisters, that I did not have to abide by his rigid rules and standards. He dominated every facet of their lives. He controlled their moods, selected their values, molded their behavior, shaped their appearances, and even told them whom they had to marry. But I also felt a great sense of loss for not getting the chance to know my father better. Although all of his children feared him, and some, like Keiko, had wished he were dead, everyone agreed that he was an exceptionally proud, intelligent, and perceptive man who had an abundance of knowledge and pride to impart to his children.

Papa was known among the Issei to be one of the last holdouts in the Japanese American frontier, a traditionalist who rigidly imposed strict Japanese standards on his children. The other Issei had come to realize that they couldn't expect their children to be Japanese, not if they lived in America. But I think that if Papa had survived, he would have eventually accepted the Americanization that was taking place among his children. There was no other choice. He would have had to accept the changes or lose the family unity he fought so hard to keep.

6

The Graveyard

*W*e left Hana's at about four-thirty when the afternoon sun had lost its scorching intensity but still had the capacity to brighten up the steel-blue sky that cast sheets of brilliant rays across the Liberty landscape. Before heading back to Sacramento, we bought a bouquet of assorted flowers and headed for the cemetery.

"Daddy's tombstone is in the *Nihon-jin* [Japanese] section," Keiko said, but I could have guessed where without her directions. Above the flat tombstones rose a cluster of tall granite headstones, the kind that the Japanese seemed to prefer. Generally, the taller the headstone, the greater the stature of the deceased in the community. Papa's was one of the most impressive, which was evidence that there were always exceptions to the rule.

Keiko placed our flowers next to a bouquet of freshly cut, long-stemmed roses. "Nesan must have been here earlier today," she said. "She comes at least once a week, prays at the Yamaguchi's grave, then at Papa's." The early morning fishing trip had turned out to be a triple catastrophe for Nesan, the icy water of the San Joaquin River snatching the lives of Papa, of her husband, and of her father-in-law when their fishing boat was capsized by an unexpected gale. The only consolation was that her eldest son had miraculously survived the accident, staying afloat with the help of the air that was trapped in his canvas jacket.

Keiko slowly walked past the tombstones, occasionally skimming her fingertips over the tops of the smooth, cool granite, stopping at one stone to inspect the dates more closely. "Mrs. Haruko Nishimoto, 1894 to 1975. She was my *baishaku-nin* [go-between]. By the time I got married, it was just a formality to have a *baishaku-nin.* But when Nesan, Hana, and Chieko got married, she performed many duties, such as helping with the wedding plans, checking out the other family's background, intervening in times of crisis."

She moved on to the next tombstone: "Mr. Sakata. He was Dad's best friend. There used to be three brothers—millionaires. Everybody in Liberty knew them. They were so rich that they had home movies. Mr. Sakata wore diamond rings. And I remember their couch. When you sat down: PPRRRUMPHH! You sank like a lead weight. But one tragic thing happened after the other. One brother was murdered, the other died of some illness, and Mr. Sakata, whatever he did, failed. People were saying, 'He must be completely out of funds by now,' but the next thing you know, he's building a new home. And people remarked, 'My! He must've had scads of money because after all those losses, he's still building a new home.'

"One morning, right after the house was built, it caught on fire with a kerosene stove—nothing was left but a pile of ashes. That day, Mrs. Sakata came to our house while Mr. Sakata was out looking for a place to stay. We couldn't put them up—there was no room.

"Mrs. Sakata just sat there in our kitchen. She didn't shed a tear! Mom said, 'What a woman of courage! To lose everything and sit there so calmly.' We cooked lunch for them, and I could still see her, sitting there, quietly eating without a trace of distress.

"Mr. Sakata told Dad, 'You know, when I was rich, we had friends that wouldn't let us rest. They'd visit morning and night, bring me gifts. At Christmas time our porch was piled up so high with *shoyu* [soy sauce], rice, and *sake* [rice wine] that we couldn't walk through. But when things started to go bad for me and people thought that I didn't have a cent left, not one of them came to visit me. They all abandoned me. But you, Tanaka-san, you are the only true friend I have.' Dad always said, 'You don't make friends just for their money.'"

Keiko edged her way between the tombstones until she came across another familiar name. "Ahh, I remember Mrs. Ito. She was a widow with several kids. She used to come over all the time when we lived at the Shimono's ranch. And Mr. Ida, you know the *tofu-ya-san* [tofu vender] who had a constant twitch in his right eye? He'd come along and flirt with her. He'd rub her ass and she'd let out a loud cackle, and after she left, Mom would say, 'I want you children to realize that if a man rubs your *oshiri* [buttocks] like that, take it as an insult! He doesn't think very highly of you. If he respects you, he won't go around rubbing your *oshiri!*'

"After Kozo [third eldest son] died, this woman came over again. She said that every time she came to visit, she used to see this rolling ball of fire either coming to or leaving our house. After Kozo died, she stopped seeing it, so she said something was coming to get him. Mom was so upset at that woman. She was furious! I guess she was insinuating that the devil was after him. But how could that be? Kozo was just a kid when he died—four years old. Hiroji [second eldest son] was the same age when he died a year earlier. I don't remember them well—they were both older than I."

Keiko kicked her sandals off and sat on a grassy knoll not far from Papa's grave. The late afternoon sunlight illuminated the entire graveyard, the tombstones sparkling like miniature granite islands in a sea of yellow-green grass. She leaned back, cupping her hands behind her head, dreamily looking up at the flock of sparrows heading north, at the trail of puffy clouds left by a single-engine plane. "You know, when I was a kid, I would lie down in the grass and dream, looking up at the clouds. I used to think, what would it be like if Dad were to disappear? He seemed to get in the way of progress, a constant threat to our security. Then when he died . . . I felt a strange sense of both release and guilt."

Keiko fell silent, her eyes scanning the sky and coming to rest on Papa's grave. "It seemed appropriate that Dad died fishing. The oldtimers used to call him the fishing professor because he always knew when and where the fish would bite. He knew the rivers backwards and forwards; he knew the tide tables; he used to read the calendar—he knew.

"People would come over and wait in line, consult with him, ask him where to go. And Dad would be very cagey with his knowledge. Occasionally, he'd tell a guy to go to the wrong place, but with a person he really liked, he'd lead him to the choicest spots."

Keiko chuckled to herself and sat up, brushing off the grass that had left slivers of indentations on her arms. "Remember Mr. Ida?" she asked, pointing to a tomb several yards away. "He was big on fishing, but the dumb klutz didn't know where to go. Dad would negotiate: 'Give me some *tofu* [bean cake] and *okara* [bean curd refuse] and I'll show you.' During the Depression he fed the entire family by fishing alone. We ate it every way imaginable—broiled, steamed, raw, poached, boiled, baked, fried—for breakfast, lunch, and dinner, seven days a week.

"One of Dad's favorite fishing partners was Nii-san (Nesan's husband). He really liked Nii-san and quite often he'd take him and Nii-san's father fishing. The Yamaguchis had a homemade boat and Dad took them to places nobody knew about. Dad would come home and demonstrate how Nii-san would get so excited because he was catching fish hand over fist that he'd almost fall out of the boat, and how the *ojii-san* [grandfather—Niisan's father] would go, 'Ssshew-ssshew, sshew, sshew,' when the fish started biting. Those were some of the happiest times for Dad because he was king. Nobody questioned his authority—he was famous for his knowledge."

Papa always managed to catch fish even when others returned empty-handed. But on that day it was different. "All four of them (Papa, Nii-san, Nii-san's father and son) had piled into that small boat," Keiko lamented. It was an unlucky day; they didn't catch anything and they were coming home when strong wind and current capsized their boat. The river was so wide and deep and the currents so swift and cold, that swimming to safety was impossible. "*Shikkari shite* [hold tightly]," Papa yelled to the others as they desperately held on to the side of the boat. Papa was the last one to go under while Nii-san's father was the first with Nii-san following after to save him, never to surface again. When they dredged Papa's body up from the river's bottom, his hands were still curled tightly, clutching his last hope. Papa always told Kenji that he'd die with his boots on—his life style and character demanded that he would.

The funeral was one of the largest that Liberty had seen with approximately a thousand mourners in attendance since the Yamaguchis were one of the most prominent members of the community. It was a calm, bright, sunny morning, very much like the one on that fateful day.

"At the funeral, I knew it was appropriate for me to cry but my tears were trapped," Keiko said, gazing in the direction of Papa's and Nii-san's tombstones that stood side by side. "What made me finally cry was when I saw Nesan. She looked like she was in a state of shock, her face sallow, a wild expression in her eyes. She let out a deep, excruciating sob, the kind that comes from deep within the pit of your stomach and wrings at your heart." Nesan was only thirty years old with five children, the oldest nine and the youngest still an infant.

"We buried Dad in the suit that he bought for Naomi's [third eldest daughter's] wedding," Keiko continued. "A white shirt that was turning yellow—the only dress shirt he owned—and a royal blue necktie. It was my idea that Dad wear his wool plaid Pendleton shirt underneath his suit. Jim (Chieko's husband) had bought it for him and it was his pride and joy—his Sunday threads.

"Kenji said that in death, Dad should go in style and he decided to buy a $600 headstone. Some of the elders could not see spending that much money. But Kenji stood fast and ultimately he got his way—everybody knew he would."

Keiko was willing to wager that something had told Papa he didn't have long to live. "He felt so rushed to tell us everything.

Rushed!" she recalled, her brows knitting into a frown. "Especially during his drinking bouts he'd weep and tell us, 'I really love you kids and I want to teach you everything I can right now because I know that time is short.' He'd get livid when he thought that we weren't absorbing his teachings and he'd yell, 'You're just repelling it like rain off an umbrella!' And he'd warn us, 'There's going to be a time in your life when you recall things I taught you and you'll know that I told you the truth. If you are a slob, only your parents will tell you because others aren't going to help you change your ways. Even if you are a dumb cluck, a parent takes the time to teach you these lessons because he loves you, cares for your well-being, feels responsible for your character. Just because I drink and have a few bad habits, just because I'm not rich, it doesn't mean that there is no truth to what I say. If I didn't love you, I wouldn't tell you these things.' He'd go on like this, over and over again, until I was choking on my dinner. I'd think to myself, 'What the hell is he yelling and screaming at us for if he loves us?' Then, as though he had read my mind, he'd say, 'I'm screaming and yelling because I love you and it's a family chore. I have to tell you this because no one else is going to tell you and time is short. *Tanin* [nonrelatives] don't care whether you have manners or not. *Tanin* don't care if you are a failure or not. *Tanin* aren't going to tell you anything. *Tanin* don't care. But I do! You'll see. Some day, all my teachings will pay off.' "

The recollection of Papa's fiery sermons seemed to tire Keiko as she lay back on the grassy knoll and gazed up at the sky where a single sparrow zigzagged across the blue, looking for the rest of his flock. "After Dad died we used to speculate about whether he had gone to heaven or not," she said, watching the sparrow until it disappeared from sight. "Mom said there was no doubt in her mind that he did. Mom had nothing but nice things to say about him. And I must have made her sad when I told her to leave him. I said, 'Why cling to him? If he wants his freedom, let him have it.' But she would get sad when I said things like that. And I couldn't understand why she would defend him."

Keiko understood Mama's feelings now, for although Keiko

had only two children and had marketable skills to support her family as a single parent, she still procrastinated for years before leaving Ted. Nobody could have ever convinced Mama that she and the children would be better off without Papa. She reasoned that despite all of Papa's shortcomings and the suffering he inflicted, he was still our father, an irreplaceable figure that kept the family together. "You children are young and impetuous," she'd tell them when they'd exhort her to leave Papa. "No matter if he drinks or gambles, he is still your father."

About a month before Papa died, Keiko remembered pleading with him. "Please don't touch the money that Mom and I made. You could go away like you said you want to—strike out on your own. I can take care of Mom and the family now." For the first time in Papa's life, he was speechless. He had no words of rebuke or anger. He just sat there and cried. Although Papa may have expressed a desire to leave the family during moments of frustration and rage, I don't think he ever had the intention to follow through with his threats. The family gave him stability, a sense of identity, belonging, and purpose.

"Mom must have cried too," Keiko conjectured. "She must have. She was going through her change of life so it must have been hard on her. After Dad died, I knew she was lonely because she really treasured his belongings . . . and I told her not to love him." Keiko bit her lower lip and stared pensively at Papa's grave. "It was only after his death that I realized that she did. I could tell by the way she kept fondling his things. She didn't want to part with them: his old underclothes, a pocket watch, and a tattered wallet. She cherished the thin silver ring that Kenji had made for Dad out of a quarter . . . Dad used to pretend it was his wedding ring."

Keiko stood up and brushed herself off. "We better get going," she said, heading for the car. The sun was slowly sinking toward other lands, leaving a blaze of orange, red, and gold in its path. I walked over to Papa's grave and kneeled before the smooth, glistening granite to pay my respects. I was glad that Kenji finally got his way—Papa would have been proud of the elegant stone that stood out prominently among the others.

"Poor Dad," Keiko whispered softly. "He had such grandiose ideas, big dreams, but he died a frustrated and tortured man. He wanted his freedom and ironically, he got it."

1

Hana

After leaving Keiko's, I stayed with Hana for a few days before returning to Los Angeles. She had taken time off from the beauty parlor and her beautician job so we could talk, and talk we did every waking hour of the day. Occasionally, her husband Ray drifted into the room, sometimes to watch the television and snooze on the easy chair or grab another cup of the black coffee perpetually brewing on the stove.

At first, I was perplexed as to why Hana left her husband of seventeen years to marry Ray. Ray looked like the stereotypic red-necked Southerner, the kind that hated everyone but the whites born in his part of town. Always sporting a cowboy hat and boots, he had critical, piercing blue eyes set in a pale white face turned red from the sun, an ever-present cigarette glued to his thin lower lip surrounded by a two-day-old stubble, and a protruding beer belly supported by skinny legs not used to exercising. His mouth barely moved when he spoke, his Texas twang slurring one word into the next, making it difficult for me to understand him. A twinkle in his eye and a slight curl to his lips gave me the cue that he had just cracked a joke, the punchline to which I always missed.

"Ray's an imposing figure, an intimidatin' man," Hana boasted. "No one dares disagree with 'im. They're too scared." But the one quality that I'm sure impressed her most was his generosity. If I cast an admiring look at any of his possessions, I soon found myself its new owner. And when it came to food, Ray insisted that Hana feed me nothing but the best.

If I was at first mystified as to why Hana had left her husband and married Ray, the reason became increasingly clear to me before I left. In many ways Ray was very much like Papa. In Hana's mind he was decisive, dominating, generous, and strong, whereas her former husband Art was wishy-washy, submissive, stingy, and weak. Those very characteristics of Art's became points of contention during their seventeen-year marriage.

It was in camp (during World War II) that the Fujimotos came to ask for Hana's hand in marriage to their eldest son Art. Mama felt a little relieved because Hana used to threaten Mama that she wouldn't get married. She would yell, "I hate to cook! I hate to sew! I hate to clean!" And Mama would say, "Shhh! Don't say things like that or nobody will come and ask for you!" Hana began to worry that she would be a burden on the family because she knew that until she got married the younger sisters couldn't. Japanese tradition dictated that rule.

Hana peeked at Art, who sat perfectly still as his mother and father did the talking.

"He wasn't what you'd call ugly," Hana recalled, "but I thought he looked like a dull, square creep. He wanted to marry me that day and I could see that Mom and Dad thought he was good for me, so I didn't say no. The next thing I know, they had me all hitched up." Hana was too afraid of Papa to object to the marriage. As she claimed later, "Even if it was someone who made me want to puke, I think I'd 've married him just to please Dad."

Papa thought the Fujimotos were *tochimochi* (land rich), which they were, so he never figured that Hana would be moving into a situation where her living conditions would be worse. Soon after the wedding Hana was given clearance to leave camp to join Art in Michigan, where he had special permission to work. But when the war was over and the Japanese Americans were allowed to return to the West Coast, Hana and her husband moved back to the family farm in Florin to live with his parents and his three brothers and sister.

She soon discovered that although Art was the eldest son, he was not given the eldest son's respect or privileges. His father would constantly remind him, "If it wasn't for me, you wouldn't be able to eat!" Art would listen with his eyes downcast.

"I realized then that I was just a slave," Hana said. "Art wasn't strong enough to have a foot in the home. And in order to feel proud, like I was doin' my part and earnin' my keep, I had to work hard. I wouldn't let anyone outwork me. I had to work to do his part for him too 'cause they were always complainin' that he's slow. I felt obligated that they're feedin' him and me—that's why I worked twice as hard."

While everyone still lay asleep, Hana arose at five o'clock and started breakfast for the family before trudging out to the strawberry fields with the rest of them. When noon came, she returned early to prepare lunch while the men washed up and sat down to be served. After eating, Hana washed the dishes while the men relaxed, finishing the kitchen chores just in time to join them back in the fields. This ritual repeated itself for dinner, six to seven days a week.

Hana had never worked harder in her life. "It was living hell," she said, "crawling in the strawberry patch all day long." Her back ached constantly and she lost more than ten pounds. Her in-laws would insinuate that since she had come from such a poor family being married must be like going from hell to heaven. Angered by their remarks she once shot back, "Father used to take us on vacation, and we took a cab, and in Bodega Bay we went fishing, and Father rented a boat."

Her father-in-law smirked. "No wonder your family was poor. Renting a cab and going fishing. No wonder they were poor."

When the family moved back to the West Coast from Arkansas and Mama went to visit Hana, she was appalled to find her daughter so gaunt and lifeless. When the attention rested on Art, Mama pulled Hana out to the barn where they could talk alone. "Hana-chan, what's wrong? You're so thin. There's some problem, isn't there? You're suffering, aren't you?" Hana just stood there, her eyes welling with tears. "Come now. Tell me everything. That's what mothers are for."

Hana just shook her head and cried even harder. She desperately wanted to spill her heart out to Mama, who was always so understanding and loving, but instead she swallowed hard to push the food back down her throat and decided to lie. "Oh, Mama, they're so good to me. No, it's not that at all." Hana knew that Mama, herself, had to endure so much suffering that she wanted to spare Mama from more.

Sunday visits to see her own family were the only outings Hana could take without feeling guilty about the time she spent away from her chores. But those visits invariably turned out to be unpleasant because Papa spent the entire time criticizing Art.

One of the things that irked Papa the most was the frugal lifestyle of Art and his family. Hana remembered how livid he'd get when she would come over and he'd see how she was dressed. "I used to wear old clothes all the time and put patch over patch," Hana recalled. "The men got to buy new clothes 'cause they shouldn't be seen like that, but the kids and me, we weren't supposed to."

That made Papa furious. He would lecture to her: "Now you're married into that family so you have to go by their rules, but I'm against having to wear rags seven days a week. It does something to people both physically and mentally if they don't try to dress up in Sunday clothes once in awhile and look neat and clean." Papa himself was always as neatly dressed as his pocketbook would allow, and he would never permit his children or wife to step foot out of their bedrooms without being properly groomed.

"I know you're married to that family and you have to go by their rules," he'd reiterate to her. "But I want to tell you one thing. You owe it to your kids! Now I want you to start putting on Sunday clothes and make them look nice one day out of the week!"

As the preaching and advice escalated to ridicule and contempt, Hana became more defensive about her husband. "I didn't think he was so hot myself," Hana remembered with renewed anger, "but it still hurt my feelings 'cause he was my husband. I thought to myself, 'He wasn't my choice. I didn't pick him out! Dad picked 'im, then he has the *gall* to keep criticizin' him!' "

One day when the criticism was particularly cruel, Hana fought back: "By God, it seems like he's all right when you come to borrow money so you can gamble. All you do all the time is criticize, criticize, criticize!"

Papa's face turned white. "Get the hell out of the house and never come back. I don't ever want to see you again!" He shouted, throwing Hana out the door, his rage beyond control, his wounded pride painfully exposed for the entire family to see. That was the first time any of his daughters had talked back to him with such insolence, especially in front of the other children, and moreover, Hana was not supposed to let Mama know that he had borrowed money from the Fujimotos.

Hana ran home crying, holding back the tears when she stepped inside the front door until she could find the safety of her bedroom. Throughout the night she sobbed, muffling her cries in the pillow as Art lay fast asleep. At four o'clock she began to panic, knowing that in another hour everyone would be getting up to work in the strawberry fields. The headache that was pounding all night now felt as though every artery in her brain was about to burst. She staggered to the bathroom to wash her face and was aghast at the vision staring back at her in the mirror. Her eyes looked like puffy red slits; her lips were cracked and swollen; her hair clung to her head, stringy and wet from perspiration and tears; and the anger that still besieged her added to the frightfulness of her appearance.

Hana tried to go back to sleep but she couldn't; the thought of going back to tell Papa off kept ringing loudly in her ears. Out of desperation she clasped her hands together and began to pray to God. As she prayed harder, something strange started to happen. "Something touched me," she said. "I had the funniest sensation from the top of my head to the tip of my toes. God touched me. You want to know what He told me?" Hana asked. " 'Love your Dad. He is hurtin' more than you.' And all of a sudden I began to realize that I was bad, lyin' there and thinkin' about goin' back and tellin' my Dad off. Oh, my goodness! That's right! God made me realize I was just thinkin' about myself."

Suddenly, a peaceful calm swept over her and she felt as though she had slept all night. She got up and went to the bathroom to get ready for the day and when she looked in the mirror found her face rested and glowing. The swelling had miraculously disappeared along with her headache.

Hana didn't tell anyone about that experience for fear they would think she was crazy, but after that morning, she had a different outlook. "Sometimes the truth is not what you hear and see. Dad showed me anger. Kicked me out. It was the only thing he could do to save his pride. But inside he was hurtin' bad."

Hana returned to apologize to Papa and Mama hurriedly dug out the money from one of her secret hiding places to return to the Fujimotos. Although Papa hesitantly accepted Hana's apology, things were never the same between them.

According to Hana, the entire incident was only symptomatic of Papa's larger problem. "He was losin' authority," she lamented. "He saw the time comin' when the kids wouldn't listen to him. When we were little we were naive, not old enough to know his faults. But when we grew older we knew, and he knew we knew. I'm sure he hated himself and he had finally come face-to-face with the fact that he was a failure."

The years had only brought with them a loss of hope and confidence that he could ever turn his dreams into reality. The last vestige of control left in his power was the tremendous grip he held over his children, but that too was gradually slipping away. And perhaps that loss was the greatest one of all because from his children he garnered his strongest sense of self-esteem and worth. Although he was criticized by some for his drinking and gambling, and admired by others for his wit, humor, and showmanship, he always received the highest praise for the way his children were raised. "No one would suspect that I'm the way I am inside the house [that is, a strict disciplinarian with his children]," he would muse. Outsiders generally regarded Mama as the one responsible for rearing and disciplining the children, but Papa said he didn't care if she received all the credit because mothers should be thought of in that way.

Perhaps the last hope that Papa had of returning to Japan a wealthy man lay with the Chinese restaurant he owned before the war. Papa won the restaurant over a gambling table from his best friend Sakata-san, and soon after he took over the business began to boom. According to Kenji, the restaurant used to gross as much as $400 to $600 a night. But prosperity abruptly came to an end when one evening two federal agents entered the restaurant and arrested Papa for gambling and selling liquor without a license.

When I asked Hana about the incident, she remembered it well. "We were selling *unkappe*. You know what that is? Chinese liquor," she explained. "These oldtimers come and they eat Chinese food and drink this *unkappe*. We didn't have a license to sell liquor so Dad always used to say that if we ever got caught—and he had the bottles hidden upstairs—to say we had to go upstairs because we had personal things we wanted to take care of, 'cause they wouldn't bother women who said that.

"So sure enough, one day here come these Federal guys. They walked right in and my God! I knew right then and there. He said he knew that we were sellin' liquor. He was lookin' around in the kitchen and he started goin' upstairs, so I ran right to the stair and I started goin' up ahead of 'im. I said, 'I have panties and things that I have to take care of.' He just shoved me out of his way and went right on up. He was checkin' the upstairs but meanwhile Mom already had the bottles and she took them down the alley in the back. She hid them out in the back there somewhere but they found the bottles."

According to Mama, every business had gambling in the back and sold liquor without a license but with the implicit consent of the police. Papa had given one of the officers $100 and told him to split it with the other, a practice that he had engaged in regularly with the local law enforcement officers. But because of that act, Papa was arrested and charged with bribing a Federal officer.

On the day of his hearing, Papa brought all of his children to court, thinking that the judge might be more lenient when he saw all nine of them. But the ploy didn't work; the judge sentenced him to fifteen years in San Quentin.

Papa spent a year in prison before he was paroled with the assistance of some Christian people who felt that he had received too severe a sentence for the offense he had committed. His release couldn't have been sooner for that year spent in prison must have been a low point in Papa's life when he had to fight for survival among murderers, thieves, rapists, drug addicts, and other hardened criminals. Perhaps the only positive aspect he could extract from the experience was that he had time to study English and had become quite fluent. He also learned the practice of *moxa* from an Issei inmate who was a specialist. He later applied this knowledge to himself, Mama, and other Issei in the Liberty community who would come for his help.

Papa wrote home quite frequently while he was incarcerated. There wasn't much else to do and Papa always did pride himself for his writing ability. One of the more memorable letters described the homosexuality in prison. "Mom was shocked to learn that those men used each other to satisfy themselves," Hana recalled. Hana also remembered Mama reading Papa's letters and saying, "Papa keeps saying there's going to be war, there's going to be war between Japan and the U.S. Be prepared. There's going to be war." Ridden with fear, Mama and Nesan burned Mama's school diploma and other tangible evidence that linked the family closely with Japan. Six months later, Japan bombed Pearl Harbor; four months after that, the United States government started to intern the first of 120,000 people of Japanese ancestry into concentration camps located in desolate parts of the country, where most were kept for the duration of the War.

When Papa left San Quentin he joined the family in Rohwer, Arkansas, one of the ten camps hastily constructed by the government. Armed guards were a familiar sight to Papa as the car drove him through the barbed wire gates into the barracks. "The car came right to our block," Hana recalled. "It stopped and out stepped Daddy, blastin' off and sayin' his piece."

Everyone was curious about Papa. The older ladies would ask Hana, "Where was your dad?" And she would make up some sort of lie to feed their curiosity. Gossip was endemic and rumors rampant in the cramped confines of the barracks with privacy invaded and family drama and individual lives exposed for others to see.

Hana remembered the adulterous affair carried on between the chef and a nurse at the hospital where she worked as an attendant. "They were caught in the act of doing it in a room where they put people with highly infectious diseases," she recalled. "I guess they thought nobody would catch 'em in there." But keeping a secret as smoldering as that was difficult in camp, and after a while the two lovers dispensed with discretion. "In the mess hall she would sit and wait on 'im and they'd act like two teenage lovers," Hana remembered. "When the chef's daughter came to the table, the woman would move to the far end. The daughter would glare at the two and make the father uncomfortable. Maybe her mother put her up to it—she knew about the affair and was probably brokenhearted."

Papa gave no occasion for getting himself caught up in the web of camp gossip, though he immediately busied himself with making bootleg liquor. He practiced his songs and magic act, and soon built a reputation as a talented entertainer. In constant demand, he was pulled from block to block to sing and perform in the various talent shows. On other days he would go looking for a poker game or sit around with his Issei cronies drinking and reminiscing about "the good old days" in Japan and California. I'm sure that during those moments with the men, he must have expressed the cynicism and anger that had been building within.

Papa was embittered by the injustices committed against people of Japanese ancestry and even more disgusted with the young Nisei who acted so American. "Cut it out," he'd admonish those Nisei speaking English. "No matter what you think, you're Japanese! Look at you Nisei! You are citizens, but still you're in here!"

According to Kenji, "People of every age bracket, especially

Nisei in their early twenties, became rebels, rowdy and irrespon-
sible—like men without a country. We all belonged to gangs,"
he recalled, "or it was unsafe. At football games or baseball, a
fight was the conclusion of the game." He particularly remembered Buster Higa, the leader of the older teenagers who used
to roam around in groups. "They hated Dad," Kenji recalled.
"They hated him because he'd wade right into their circles and
try to educate them about being Japanese. One time they ganged
up on him and broke one of his ribs."

Papa never forgot the humiliation. After the war ended and
he returned to Liberty, he went looking for Buster Higa with
Kenji at his side. "Remember when you guys worked me over?"
he asked. "Let's finish it off right here!" he challenged. Higa got
on his knees and begged for forgiveness.

When the army came to recruit the young Nisei in camp, these
boys were probably some of the first to volunteer to prove their
loyalty as American citizens. Papa probably questioned their
logic and snickered at the irony of fighting for America while
their families remained in camp, especially since some of those
boys never returned.

Ted Takemoto, a Liberty-born Nisei, was one of them. His
mother awakened in the middle of the night because she heard
her son calling for her. The next morning when a telegram
arrived, she didn't have to open it. She knew what it said. Before
he had left for overseas, she had run around desperately trying
to find women, born in the year of the tiger, to tie a knot in a
cloth that she would wrap around her son's stomach to ward away
the bullets. But the protection it was suppose to give didn't work,
or maybe he forgot to wear it that particular day because now he
was dead. Killed in combat.

When the first chance to get out of the camps arrived, Papa
jumped at it. "There was a *Nihon-jin* [Japanese] family that had
a job at a big resort, Whispering Sands, right there in Florida,"
Hana recalled. "We got the job through them. I don't know what
the deal was but we heard that it was money-making." Papa went
as a gardener, Hana was the waitress, and Naomi the dishwasher.
The rest of the family stayed in camp.

The trip from Arkansas to Florida was quite a memorable one for Hana. "When the bus stopped in Louisiana, I didn't know which bathroom to go to," she chortled. "I thought, 'We are Japanese and they don't like us so I guess we're supposed to go to the toilet on the black side.' I was just standing around trying to find a toilet and a guy in there told me that I was in the wrong place. I was to use the white side."

Papa, Hana, and Naomi were waiting at the depot for a train when the police descended in a squad car and arrested Papa. "Someone turned us in saying that they saw a Japanese man and they knew by lookin' at 'im that he was a spy." Hana laughed. "Dad was really a sharp-lookin' man," she offered as an explanation for their suspicion. "He just sat there and looked everyone up and down. They finally let us go because we all had proper papers."

The opulence they met at the Whispering Sands was a startling contrast to the barren camps they left behind. Women, their arms dripping with jewelry, and men sunbathed on the white sandy beaches while uniformed waiters served them exotic, tropical drinks and fancy hors d'oeuvres. Romance flourished and rumors abounded with the arrival and departure of new and old guests.

One guest that Hana remembered quite vividly was a short, round-faced divorcee in her mid-fifties. "I liked her," Hana said. "She was a Russian woman, blunt and frank. She wore fake jewelry but when there were parties, she'd go to the safe and bring out her real McCoys. She'd always warn me, 'Don't take in a young thing 'cause you can't trust 'em.'" At her side stayed a mean black mongrel dog that wouldn't let anyone come near. The dog was her constant companion. Her husband had left her for a young girl: a runaway, the woman explained, poor, dirty, hungry-looking, and sad. The woman took her into her home, gave her a job as a housekeeper, then one day found her husband in bed with her.

Despite the abundance at the resort, Papa was unhappy the minute he arrived. He had taken an instant dislike to Sachi, the eldest daughter of the family who was responsible for getting them their jobs. She appeared to be friendly—fat and jolly—but Papa kept warning Hana and Naomi, "Watch out for that woman. She's evil."

Without any gambling or friends to occupy his time, Papa must have spent a lot of time alone brooding about his lot in life, dreaming about better days, and scheming up plans to get even if not ahead. He was probably even more disgruntled because the war had forced him to come face to face with his decision that he was never going home. He had answered "yes" to question 28 in the "loyalty questionnaire" administered to the entire evacuee population, which stated that he would " . . . forswear any form of allegiance or obedience to the Japanese emperor, or any foreign government, power, or organization." Although this question was later changed for the Issei to read, "Will you swear to abide by the laws of the United States to take no action which would in any way interfere with the war effort of the United States?" Papa had made up his mind that he would never return to Japan.

But the possibility of "striking it rich" never left his dreams. In one of the letters he wrote to Mama in camp, he described in vivid detail the circumstances of the sudden fortune he had become heir to. It went something like this: "We're going to be rich! Rich! I was walking along the beach when I heard someone crying for help. I looked toward the water and spotted a head bobbing up and down about 100 feet from shore. I quickly slipped off my shoes and dove into the water and rescued this woman who was practically unconscious when I dragged her ashore. I recognized the woman as the rich widow who had a permanent suite at the resort. She was so grateful I saved her life that she drew up a will giving all her riches to me. After being ill for a very short time, she died."

Mama was so elated. She put down the letter and told Kenji, who wanted in on the good news. With the younger children impatiently tugging at her sleeves to eat at the mess hall, she tucked the letter back in the envelope and waited for a quiet time when she could finish reading it. After lunch she rushed back to the barracks: "Her lawyers called me to the office," the letter continued, "and they were about to hand over a large sum of money, when I woke up. It was all a dream."

Papa probably lived a very rich life of fantasy both in his dreams and while awake. Like most good actors who excel at their craft, he was an expert on human nature, spending hours studying people's mannerisms and behavior and second-guessing their motives and character traits. The one advantage he had of being a gardener at the resort was that he could quietly work, listen, and observe without arousing suspicion. Perhaps they thought he couldn't understand English, but whatever the case, his presence didn't matter to them because he was totally outside of their social sphere of significant others.

After his work day ended, Papa would from time to time send Hana out to buy him a bottle of wine. Once, while out on such a mission, Hana remembered the embarrassment she faced. "I was with that lady, Sachi, and her two sisters who hated Pop, so when I went into a place to buy some wine, I hid it under my jacket. Here we were, shoppin' around, and I was followin' them and just when we were ready to go home, that ol' bottle slipped out, busted on the floor and stank the whole place up. I wasn't about to go home without it 'cause I knew Dad was waitin' for me, so I went out and got another, but I could just hear 'em sayin', 'Look at that old man—the kid is buyin' wine for him!'"

Although the sisters did not like Papa, one thing they could never complain about was his work. In no time he had the grounds well manicured and ablaze with brilliant, annual flowers. "We were all makin' good," said Hana who recalled earning approximately $100 a week—far more than the $10.50 allowance they received in camp. But as the friction between Papa and Sachi escalated, so did Papa's discontent. One morning Papa packed his few belongings and headed back to join the rest of the family in camp, leaving Hana and Naomi behind with the same warning, "Watch out for that evil woman."

Before Hana and Naomi returned to camp, they were to find much substance to Papa's warnings. "We discovered she was a two-timing, scheming woman," Hana said. "She wanted the cook's job and got him fired. When the owner came, she told on the manager and got him fired too. She got the manager's confidence, then ratted on him, telling the owner how his girlfriend was there all the time eatin' the food. Dad was right. She was bad."

Hana was elated when Papa left because with his discontent, he had made life miserable for her and Naomi. "There were times I hated him," Hana declared. "But when Dad was happy, there wasn't a man in the world who made little things more joyous. He sings. He acts. He jokes. When he wants to celebrate, oh, was it festive! He invites people over and he starts cookin' and we kids all had to get in there and help him cook." Hana began to laugh thinking about Papa. "He's so excited and enthused. And he brags and carries on about how good a cook he is and how Mom doesn't know how to cook. He jokes and teases her and makes her laugh til she pees in her pants."

After mustering up a serious face, Mama would say, "I let him brag. I don't care. I hate to cook anyway. Why, if I could spend the kind of money he does on his cooking, I could cook just as well as he."

Hana's laughter and mine spilled into the living room, where Ray had fallen fast asleep on the easy chair. "I tell you, Dad was a very exciting man," Hana continued. "He's the kind that 'd try anything once. I remember in camp he used to eat rattlesnake meat whenever he got drunk. When he'd go to the ocean he'd pick up anything that's crawlin' and say it's good. We ate mussels, spoon turtle, catfish, sardines, snails, pigeons, jackrabbits, mustard greens—you name it, we ate it. He never made us feel like we were eatin' those things 'cause we were poor. No! Ooh! He'd carry on like it was the greatest delicacy in the world."

Hana was deep in reverie. When I asked her what she was thinking about, she just shook her head and smiled. She was remembering Papa. "He was something else, that man," she grinned. "He really was. He had a bad side too, but there was another side of him that you can never forget." Like Keiko, Hana had a love/hate relationship with Papa, but now that he was dead and the bitter feuding had long been forgiven, only the love prevailed to color her thoughts.

8

Kenji

I had put off visiting my brother for the last, knowing that he would be the most difficult for me to talk to—not only because he was extremely busy on behalf of the religious organization with which he held an important position but also because throughout most of my adolescent years he was the father figure in my life, the person whom I feared and obeyed. I never found it easy or comfortable talking to him.

After Papa died, Kenji stepped right into his shoes, assuming the authority and responsiblities as the head of the household. He took on his new role with the grave seriousness and vigor of a beginner starting his first day at work. Many of the sisters who had to abide by his rules resented him for imposing the same rigid standards set by Papa. After all, Kenji was only a brother and yet he tried to be a carbon copy of Papa.

"Who says you have to kowtow to your older brother?" Keiko complained. "In American books we're all equal!" But according to Kenji, he was only fulfilling his role expectations. His father had always drilled it into him that as the only son he had the responsiblity of looking after his mother and sisters in the event something should happen to Papa.

In retrospect, I'm certain that if Kenji really had a choice in the matter he would have pursued his own dreams and goals rather than be saddled with the burden of supporting four younger sisters and a mother. He was only twenty-four years old when Papa died. But instead, he did stick by the family, moving all of us with him to Los Angeles, where he had secured a better job as an auto mechanic.

The many conflicts that had arisen between brother and sisters had long been healed with the understanding that comes with the passing of years when I called Kenji to set up an appointment with him. He was preparing to go on another month-long trip to Hawaii and Japan but agreed to meet me for dinner at my mother's house.

Mama had been anxiously awaiting his visit for over a week. Months had elapsed since she had seen him last. Even when she lived next to him in a little house behind his own, she rarely saw him because his job kept him traveling around the world for at least six months out of the year. His visits always managed to buoy her spirits, for among all of her children he was the most special. He was her only son.

Mama must have been relieved when Kenji was born because at last, after her first three pregnancies, she had borne Papa a male child. None of the children needed to be told that the newest member of their family was a boy. They knew by watching Papa. He was jubilant and ecstatic beyond control. Proudly, Mama held the newborn infant up for Papa to cradle in his arms. Night after night as he admired his son he tried to think of the best name he could give him. After two days he finally settled on the name Kenji: smart and healthy.

A glow of pride and reassuring comfort settled over Mama's face as she watched her son sleeping peacefully between Papa and herself. For the first time in their marriage Papa pampered her, brought her food and comfort. "I don't have to get up and do my chores," she thought to herself. "No. Not yet." She had finally proven her worth.

Kenji arrived at Mama's promptly at six o'clock with a bag full of groceries for her. He was dapperly dressed in a brown suede sport coat, brown slacks, a crisply starched white shirt, and resting slightly askew on his head was a white beret, an added flair to lend a touch of flamboyance to his lean physique. Kenji was always nattily dressed, extremely conscious of his physical appearance, just like Papa, who used to preen before the mirror each time he stepped out. Not a hair stood out of place, not a wrinkle creased his pants or shirt as Kenji made his entrance into Mama's house and greeted us as if he had seen us yesterday.

Mama sat on the couch and beamed. She was proud of her son who had worked himself up from the rank and file to become one of the top officials in a Buddhist religion boasting thousands of members. I quickly took the grocery bag and set about serving the food that I had ordered at a nearby Chinese restaurant. "I'll help myself," Kenji said, digging into the food. Kenji was never allowed to serve himself when Papa was alive; Papa wouldn't hear of it. He didn't want Kenji to do anything considered "feminine." Kenji took off his shoes, sat on the floor, and started to eat while Mama and I followed suit.

At first Kenji spoke with the cautious politeness reserved for those we rarely see, but as the evening progressed and we began to talk about Papa, his face lit up and the serious expression that earlier masked his face turned into a solid grin.

I'm sure Kenji wished that Papa were still alive to see him because in his profession he had achieved the kind of status and recognition that would have made Papa proud. He had won the respect and adoration of thousands to whom he had given guidance over the years. Members of his congregation would tell me, "Your brother is really something special. No matter how great the pressure, he's always calm and fresh as a lettuce."

Another member likened him to a magnet. "He draws people to him with his humor," she said. "He makes them laugh until their stomachs hurt." Still another remarked, "It only takes a few words for him to touch your heart. His youthful spirit, his genuine sincerity and respect and consideration for others, always shine through."

Probably one of the main motivating forces behind Kenji's achievements was his desire to please Papa, but while Papa lived Kenji could never quite measure up to his expectations. Part of the problem lay in the high expectations that Papa had for him. "He used to pound it into Kenji's head that he wanted him to bring honor and glory to the family name," Keiko said. "I guess in Dad's mind, Kenji was going to go back to Japan, carry on the family name, and avenge his father."

For four generations, the Tanaka lineage bore only one son per family, and now that Kenji was the last male of the family line the responsibility lay with him to carry forth the family name to the next generation. "In Japan, families invest everything in the *chōnan* [eldest son]," Kenji remarked. "The family's pride, glory, and future are set in the eldest son. And Dad was so proud of his family tree, his family background. His dream was to send me back to Japan to carry on that tradition."

After the two younger brothers, Hiroji and Kozo, died, Kenji's status as the eldest son became even greater. "I remember when we went to visit the grave site of the two boys," Yoko said. "Kenji just squatted there before their graves and cried."

As the eldest son, special attention and training were immediately accorded to Kenji. Every evening during supper and for thirty minutes to an hour after, all the children were instructed in matters concerning table manners, the Japanese language, values, history, and tradition. Kenji was given additional tutoring since he would represent the family during special occasions and would need to know the proper greetings and formalities that preceded and followed each occasion.

"In many ways the *chōnan* was like a pet dog," Kenji laughed. "Dad would send me places on behalf of the Tanakas and I would have to express special greetings with deep formality." Papa would smolder with impatience and try to cover up his embarrassment because Kenji couldn't accurately regurgitate what he was taught. "People knew he was hurting inside because of me," Kenji said. "But I didn't have a memory."

It must have become quickly apparent to Papa that his son could not catch on to his lessons as readily as did his older and younger sisters. "I flunked first grade three times," Kenji laughed. "Couldn't get past my ABC's. Many times I got sent home from school." Kenji blamed his learning disability on a bout with meningitis that had stricken him as a youngster. He had run a high fever for over a week and the doctors had told

Mama to start planning for the funeral.

Because of Kenji's learning disability, Papa fought even harder to instill character into his son. "I felt like I was in a military boot camp," Kenji recalled. "He used to show me how to comb my hair, how to sit, eat, walk, and sleep." If Kenji were to slouch or amble about without purpose, Papa would slap him on his back and shout, "If a soldier walked like that, they'd beat him up. Hold your head up! Walk like a man!"

Even when Kenji was sleeping, he did not escape Papa's scrutiny. Kenji said, "If I was sleeping with my legs sticking out of the covers, he'd yank the covers off and roll me out of the bed because even in my sleep, he wanted me to show decency."

Papa believed that the children needed to suffer in order to toughen their spirits and strengthen their resolve. Kenji remembered how he and the sisters would have to walk to school and home in the pouring rain, three miles up and back. "Most all of the families took and picked up their children when it rained, but not Dad. He believed that if you have to get a ride to school, your seriousness of studying weakens. We'd act like we were waiting for Dad and wait until everyone went home, then we'd run through the fields. Eventually, some of the neighbors would wait and give us a lift, dropping us off a little away from home so Dad wouldn't catch sight."

To further Kenji's character training, Papa sent him to judo lessons to learn discipline and the art of self-defense. "The eyes, the eyes! Look into the eyes of your opponent when you fight!" he would yell as he engaged Kenji in a sparring match. "And when you talk, look into the person's eyes. Don't look down at the floor. It shows weakness."

Kenji's judo training served a useful purpose because oftentimes he had to protect himself from physical harm while confronted with racial hostility and ridicule. Kenji would proudly recount his victorious battles to Papa who would judgmentally listen and conclude: "If you're gonna fight, you better win!" Papa rarely offered praise, although inside I'm sure he was proud of his son's physical prowess.

But the academic setbacks that Kenji continued to face

probably dampened the enthusiasm over any feat that Kenji could have boasted. Kenji's laughter echoed a mixture of remorse and embarrassment when he recalled the time he flunked seventh grade. "During physical education this kid called me a Jap. I told him to wait outside by the gym after school. Everyone gathered around waiting for the fight and I kicked the shit out of him. One of the girls reported on me and the next day the principal told me to go home. I came home at two o'clock and Dad wanted to know what happened. I told him how I worked this kid over because he called me a Jap. Dad got furious and he took Nesan (to help interpret) and me to the principal's office, fuming all the way. When he got there he demanded an explanation from the principal. The principal told him, "Your son is retained again for another year." Dad just stood there, a big tear rolled down his face and he turned around and went back home without saying a word."

The one aptitude wherein Kenji did show great interest concerned anything that was mechanical. "Every time he got a toy, within an hour he had it all torn apart," Hana remarked. "He wasn't satisfied until he saw how it worked." Visiting guests would often find that their cars wouldn't start when they tried to leave. Papa's eyes would dart to Kenji, knowing he had tinkered with it.

"Show us what you touched," the guest would gently coax Kenji. And Papa would get furious, but inside he probably took glee in his son's mischievous propensity. "Boys will be boys," was probably his thought, and putting anything mechanical in front of Kenji was like giving a book of matches to an arsonist.

However, on one occasion, a simple admonishment was not sufficient for the harm that Kenji's mechanical curiosity brought. "One of the workmen had a precious gold watch handed down from generation to generation," Hana recalled. "He treasured it with loving care. Somehow Kenji got hold of it and the next thing you know, it looked like an old robot with springs pokin' out every which way. Mom and Dad didn't know what to do. It was beyond repair and they didn't have the money to buy another one."

In order to let the man know how badly he felt about it, Papa tied Kenji to a tree and ordered him to stay there all night. Long after the workmen went to sleep and Mama pretended to be doing the same, Papa nudged her and said, "Don't tell Kenji I told you, but go out there and untie him. Sneak him in so he thinks I don't know."

Despite the disappointments that Papa felt about his son, a special bond and closeness was reserved only for Kenji. Papa took his son with him wherever he went, talked to him about things he never shared with his daughters, broke him in from boyhood to manhood. Papa had often told Kenji of the loneliness he had felt from not having a father, especially when he was a teenager, and he didn't want Kenji to feel the same way.

Kenji still vividly remembered the smell of the earth, the color of the sky, the fatigue in his bones on that special day in Arkansas when father and son smoked their first cigarette together after the end of a long day's work. "We took a break and squatted there in the field looking at the setting sun. Dad pulled out his pouch and rolling paper and handed it to me. 'Here, take a smoke,' he said. I refused, 'No, no,' like I never touched the stuff, but he insisted. He probably knew I was already smoking. I'll never forget that cigarette and smoking with him. A cigarette never tasted so good."

Papa was also the first one to further Kenji's sex education, even providing him with funds to pursue it. "Here, go find a whore," he grunted. "If a man masturbates, he gets stupid!" Kenji looked dumbfoundedly at the ten-dollar bill. "I don't know where to go," he said with embarrassment. Papa threw him the keys to the car and told him where to go.

One of the many excursions that Kenji took with Papa was to the gambling dens. "Mom used to send me with Pop all the time because if I didn't go, he'd be gone two, three nights." Papa would stay until the morning light and Kenji would pull himself up on the pool table and fall asleep until Papa was ready to quit. That was when Kenji was only six, seven years old.

When Kenji got old enough to drive a car, he'd drop Papa off. When he returned to pick him up, Papa would yell to the waitress. "My son's here. Set 'im up." Papa believed that if Kenji was old enough to work, he was old enough to drink. His philosophy, as far as it applied to men, was that it was all right to drink hard, fight hard, and gamble hard as long as one worked hard.

Once when Kenji came to pick up Papa, he recalled, he was met by two ruffians. Probably angered by some altercation that had transpired between them and Papa in the gambling den, they offered to fight Kenji. "I turned and kicked them in the nuts," laughed Kenji. "Dad and his buddies came out of the den and roared with laughter."

According to Kenji, many of the Japanese boarding houses and pool rooms had gambling, liquor, and women in the back rooms. The front business was only secondary to the gambling. The men would play *hana* (a Japanese card game), rummy, poker, and various Chinese games, and the stakes were often high. "Dad would gamble off a crop, the car, the store," Kenji recalled. "He'd put everything down on the table to chance bringing home enough for everyone. That's how he won the chop suey restaurant—on the gambling table. And if he lost, he never quibbled about it. He'd scrape money together and start again."

That was Papa's downfall—he'd always start again and that's when the tension and hardships would escalate. Mama would nag, scream, and cry, but Papa would head right back to the dens after finding the hiding places where she secreted money. And when all the hiding places were pillaged and only a few coins remained in the family coffers, Mama was the one who had to go out and borrow money. Papa would send her because he knew he didn't have a chance and that no one would have the heart to turn Mama down.

The only time the gambling abated and the arguments stopped was when Papa was interned in Rohwer during the war, and shortly thereafter when the family remained in Arkansas to farm. Those were some of the happiest years for Mama and the most peaceful recollections for Kenji too. Papa depended heavily upon Kenji to harvest the crop and drive it to market, but the team effort was satisfying because for the first time since coming to America the family was able to save money. Papa didn't gamble; there were no gambling dens.

Mama and Papa leased thirty acres and grew green onions, carrots, beans, tomatoes, okra, and sold them at the local markets. According to Mama, "Before we arrived [in Arkansas], the markets bought their produce from California growers, but since ours was fresher, they bought from us." Kenji remembered that on the weekends, Papa would invite the neighbors and his business associates to come over to the house and eat. He would cook up a variety of Chinese dishes and after dinner, he would crank up the phonograph and everybody danced.

Mama hated to leave Arkansas. The family prospered and the people were generous and kind. "They gave us a farewell dinner before we left," she reminisced. "The *Haku-jin* in Arkansas treated us like relatives . . . they're not like the ones here in California." But with several daughters who would soon be eligible for marriage, they knew they had to return to California; otherwise, the girls would have to marry out of their race. "Papa and I decided that we couldn't just think about ourselves—with this money we must return," Mama reasoned. "And with one truck and a station wagon, we left when we were ahead."

Papa probably couldn't contain his excitement as the car rolled into Liberty and he caught a glimpse of the main street of Japan town. With a wad of bills in his pockets and a gleam in his eyes, he headed straight for town after the family got settled. "I'm going to say hello to my buddies," he offered as an excuse, and before long, Papa was lost to the gambling dens.

As much hardship as Mama faced because of Papa's gambling, Kenji was convinced that Papa suffered even more. "He wanted to tear himself away from misfortune and the ugliness he had inside of him," said Kenji, "but he couldn't because of his addiction. He was torn between the family and the outside world and tormented inside with his two personalities of Jekyll and Hyde."

At home, Papa was like a stern preacher delivering sermons about morality and proper social graces and demanding strict discipline from his children, who all feared him. According to Kenji, Papa's rigidity in childrearing stemmed from his upbringing in Japan. He was raised by relatives in a rural village that adhered very strictly to the Confucian-derived samurai values of feudal Japan; then, after coming to America and becoming a family man himself, Papa emphasized traditional patterns even more. Perhaps it was an adaptive mechanism used by Papa to maintain his pride, to compensate for the inferior social status and limited economic opportunities imposed on immigrants of Japanese ancestry. Or perhaps it was Papa's way to maintain parental authority and family solidarity. As Papa had repeatedly told his children, "I'll never separate the family and let them suffer the pain of not being raised by their own parents." The suffering that he had experienced as a result of his father's abandonment had left an indelible scar on his mind, a grudge and hatred that grew even more intensely after his father had left him in America.

The cultural conflicts that arose because of Papa's emphasis on traditional patterns were aggravated by the fact that Papa himself didn't practice what he preached. The minute he stepped outside, his rigid, disciplined, and serious character was transformed to conviviality. He was the life of the party, the one whom all the men sought to work next to, the sport who never complained about his losses but bought a round of drinks for the men instead.

Papa thoroughly loved the festive life of drinking, gambling, and entertainment. In his younger days in Japan, he had aspired to be a performing artist. He was a favorite among the farmers of surrounding villages, who would come to hear him sing at the rice planting festivals of early spring. Before long, he caught the interest of several talent scouts who wanted to take him to Tokyo for further exposure and experience. Papa declined their offers but he probably regretted his decision, for he used to tell Kenji, "I could have made it in the entertainment field." But Papa's decision was tempered by his knowledge and regret that those in the entertainment field were never respected.

In Liberty, Papa's talents did not escape the attention of the community either. His gift with words found him eulogizing at funerals and his ability to entertain got him invited to many weddings. Kenji recalled that at weddings and parties, people waited for him to sing. "He was invited to many weddings to be the master of ceremonies, even when he didn't know the families too well. He was a humorous storyteller. He knew how to crank up the atmosphere, pick up the mood, get everyone laughing. He would sing old, classic Japanese songs and put his own creative expression and interpretation into them. He loved being out in front."

Once or twice a year professional entertainment groups from Japan would come to Liberty and charge admission to see their show. Papa never missed those shows—nobody did—they were highlights of the year. Papa would boil with anger when the groups were bad and was the first to express his dissatisfaction by hooting them off the stage. He would bristle: "How dare they take the poor farmers' money with their amateurish entertainment!"

Kenji had both Mama and me laughing when he described how Papa once went as far as physically ousting the entertainers off stage. "Dad got up and had a big brawl right there on stage," Kenji chuckled. "His shirt was ripped off and he suffered a few cuts and bruises, but he wasn't going to sit back and let them get away without letting them know how bad they were."

Papa's frustrated yearning to be a professional performing artist was probably never resolved. As many artists will testify, once the excitement of performing enters your bloodstream it never leaves. The frustrations of not realizing his own potential, of not having a nurturing childhood, and of not achieving success in America, had found expression in the strict standards he set for his children and in the compulsive gambling that consumed his life. That opportunity for him to achieve his goals, that ephemeral moment in life when all conditions were at optimum, had passed him by and only the obstacles stayed behind to remind him of his failures, of his incorrigible gambling habit, of the eleven children he had lost to America, of the Alien Land Laws and discriminatory legislation and attitudes that made it difficult for a person of Japanese ancestry to get ahead.

Papa used to blame his gambling on his father, who had indulged in the habit during his long stay in America. "During those days the Issei all liked gambling," said Mama. "Takeyama-san had a gambling hall in the back of his barber shop and Grandfather Tanaka would go gamble there. Papa would wait patiently outside . . . midnight, one o'clock . . . but still his father wouldn't come out. Papa would say, 'Let's go home, let's go home.' But his father would insist, 'Wait, wait,' and that's the way it went. That's how Papa got into gambling. His rationale was that as long as his father gambled so much, he might as well too."

After returning to America, Papa turned to gambling as the one way to achieve overnight success. Kenji said, "He knew that it would take him a lifetime of hard labor and scrimping and scraping to accumulate the kind of money he made with his father, whereas with the roll of the dice or a lucky hand, he could win two or three months' earnings in one night." Working for wages and slowly climbing up the pay scale was a distasteful option for Papa because he wanted to be his own boss. "I'll never bow my head to someone from payday to payday," Papa would tell Kenji. And if the boss didn't talk to Papa with proper respect, he would quit on the spot—even if he didn't know how he would feed his children the next day.

During the Depression when jobs were scarce, Papa would go fishing each day and sell his catch or barter it for other goods. "One thing I never did was to bring home other people's garbage to feed you," Kenji could remember Papa saying. With Kenji at his side, Papa would strut proudly into town with a toothpick in his mouth. "He wanted to show others that his stomach was full and he was well taken care of," said Kenji. He'd explain to his son, "Even if you're dying from starvation, never admit you're hungry." But in the privacy of his home, he'd openly weep before his wife and children because he couldn't educate and provide for them well.

Kenji was convinced that if Papa could only have shaken off

his gambling addiction he could have been quite a businessman. "He had a way with people, knew how to get them to do things for him," Kenji boasted. "He could even sell a truckload of rotten fruit and have the buyer thanking him for the bargain."

The end of the war marked a turning point in Papa's life. His prospects of "striking it rich" had met with disappointment and despair, and his homeland now was devastated from defeat. These factors forced on him the painful realization that he was never going home. "His pride would never have allowed him to return poor and to leach off of his relatives," Kenji lamented. "He was too proud to ever admit defeat."

Turning once again to contract farming as a means of making a living, Papa must have looked to a pretty bleak future. Now in his fifties and with his strength and stamina not sufficient to endure the long hours of hard physical labor in the fields, he began to lean more heavily on Kenji. When Kenji told Papa that he was going to Los Angeles to pursue further training in auto mechanics, Papa was vehemently against it.

"The way I left home . . . I did wrong," Kenji said, remorsefully shaking his head while recalling those memories. "I know Dad was discouraged when I left. He depended a lot on me." Papa had insisted that Kenji stay, but Mama exhorted, "Go! You must go." She knew that if Kenji didn't learn a trade, his future would be no better than Papa's.

Learning a trade became an obsession with Kenji because he had dropped out of school and had no marketable skills other than the experience he had gathered from Papa as a labor contractor. Desperate to try any option, he clipped out an ad from the local newspaper and sent away for a "learn-how-to-become-a-baker" kit.

Keiko clearly remembered the first doughnut Kenji made. "It was as hard as a brick," she laughed. "We told him they were good so he tried baking some cakes and cookies but they all turned out the same." Kenji quickly scrapped the idea of becoming a baker, but kept insisting that he must learn a trade.

"After Kenji left, Papa was lonely," Mama recalled. "He was

getting old and he no longer wanted to do contract farming. He couldn't do it by himself." I suppose that as long as he had Kenji by his side, Papa felt powerful. Kenji provided him with the kind of confidence, pride, security, and comradeship that his daughters could not supply simply because of their gender. Daughters you raised for the benefit of other people's families, but sons were cultivated for your own.

The next time Kenji and Papa saw each other again, Kenji was on his way to Korea. The Korean War had started and Kenji was one of the first to volunteer in the army. He was seated in the plane at Travis Air Force Base, ready to take off for overseas, when he looked out of the window and spotted Papa standing at the airport gate. "We both saw each other," Kenji recalled. "He just stood there, a big tear rolled down his cheek as he watched until the plane took off."

That was his last recollection of Papa because Papa was dead when Kenji came home again. He had gotten an honorable discharge from the army to help the family because of his father's demise. Keiko wrote the letter on Mama's behalf.

January 12, 1954
TO WHOM IT MAY CONCERN:
I, Michiko Tanaka, age 50, mother of Kenji Tanaka, wish to apply for a dependency and hardship discharge of my son.

The death of my husband on December 27, 1953, leaves myself and my six daughters aged 19, 17, 16, 14, 11, and 9, with absolutely no financial support other than the measly wages of my daughter, who graduated high school in 1952 and is presently earning $200.00 per month. She has just had a major operation on December 4, 1953, and is in very poor health which keeps her from work many days.

If my son should get a discharge, he would be able to provide for us as did my husband, although my son had been supporting two of his dependents before going in the army.

Our approximate month expenses run about $280.00-$290.00. We are paying $63.00 for our house, $120.00 for food, $14.00 for utilities, $26.00 per month for the children's school lunch, $35.00 for clothes, and $40.00 for miscellaneous items such as gas, etc. Of course, the above figures indicate just the *absolute necessities* to live, which certainly does not provide for us comfortably. Presently, all seven of us are living in a three bedroom home.

I certainly feel that a discharge of my son would relieve us considerably of much hardship. Please consider my urgent plea.

Mrs. Michiko Tanaka

I'm sure that when Papa gasped for his last breath before reaching unconsciousness, he felt reassured that Kenji would come home to take his place. He had come to that realization much earlier when Kenji was still a teenager.

"I was about seventeen, eighteen years old and Dad was about to lay hands on Mom, and I flipped him over on his back," Kenji recalled. "I thought he was going to get angry and strike me, but instead he just stood up, smiled at me and said, 'Ah, I could die any time now that I know I have a son who'll go to this extent to protect his mother.'"

Kenji was still in Korea when Papa was making plans for the day that his son would visit the Tanakas and the Satos in Hiroshima. Since he was stationed so close to Japan, Papa wanted him to visit both families on one of his furloughs. Papa would rehearse with Mama all the special greetings and messages he should convey. But because of Papa's untimely death, Kenji never did make that trip.

"I went and visited Papa's family," I told Kenji, who had never gone to Hiroshima despite his many trips to Japan. I started to tell Kenji more of the details of my trip but stopped when I realized he didn't seem too interested. "Someday, I'll show you all the pictures that I took of Papa's relatives, his home village, and Mama's family in Japan," I offered.

Kenji shook his head. "Nah, I don't keep pictures of anyone. Not even myself," Kenji said. "Maybe it's because I don't have any children to pass them on to."

It was ten-thirty when we finally left Mama's. Kenji seemed like he wanted to stay and talk some more about Papa, but Mama looked exhausted and I had to get home. That night was probably the first time Kenji had talked so much about Papa. There were still many stories he had to tell—about the time Papa talked a police officer out of a ticket, about Papa's drinking buddies, and more—but he was off the next morning on yet another trip and he didn't know when we could meet again.

We lingered a little while longer outside Mama's apartment building, exchanging a few words before heading our separate ways. I watched Kenji as he headed for his car. His walk was brisk, his posture erect, his head held high. He stopped briefly under the street lamp and turned to wave goodbye, well aware that I was still watching him, the last *chōnan* of the Tanaka family.

9

Going Home

Kenji knew too much. That's why he never went to visit my parents' families in Japan even though he was there more than a dozen times. He never told me this, but I suspect my guess is right. He was the Tanaka *chōnan* and he couldn't very well visit my mother's and father's families without bearing gifts, repaying past debts, and offering the proper salutations and apologies that he thought were necessary. After all, he was schooled for this visit by both Mama and Papa, who saw in their son a representative of themselves.

Just like Mama's and Papa's, his pride would not have allowed him to see the Tanakas and the Satos without doing the "right thing." As for myself, I could feign innocence and everyone would overlook my ignorance, oversights, and faux pas. After all, I was the youngest, and moreover a woman. But the expectations placed upon my brother would have been far greater. He was the *chōnan*, a position everyone would recognize, especially in Japan.

Another reason why he never made that visit to my parents' families could be that the pressure placed upon him for returning in my parents' stead no longer existed. Papa was dead. Papa was the one who made such a big deal about going home in the proper way. He had more to prove than Mama. He was a male, the head of the household, the one responsible for his family's status and welfare: the *chōnan.* And if Kenji returned, in many ways he would have to take Papa's place, doing what Papa was never able to do himself. But with Papa out of the picture and only Mama to deal with, Kenji could do as he wished. Papa was the one he always tried to please. Mama never heavy-handedly imposed her will on any of her children.

Going home. That's what most Issei thought about when they came to America. "Striking it rich" and going home was the Issei dream. But like my parents, many were to remain in America for the rest of their lives, many of the men living their last days as lonely bachelors.

When I was visiting my parents' families in Hiroshima, I often wondered what our lives would have been like if my mother and father had returned to Japan. Or what if they had never left? Of course, there was the possibility that we would not have survived the war, since Hiroshima was completely flattened by the atomic bomb on August 6, 1945. With that blast 78,000 were annihilated and another 78,000 would die over the next 43 years from its aftereffects. My mother's family store was less than a mile from the epicenter. Only three people who lived that close survived. My Aunt Istue was one of the three who lived to recount that day of infamy. The blinding light, the mushroom cloud, the searing 12,000-degree Fahrenheit heat, the house collapsing around her, then the black rain: those were images she could never forget when the bomb fell at eight-fifteen that morning.

Somehow she managed to pull herself out of the ruins and amidst the moaning, the cries for help, and the chanting of *"Nam-myoho-renge-kyo,"* she staggered to the river where many victims sought refuge. She looked with horror at the survivors whose flesh dripped off their bodies, not knowing that she looked as ghastly as they. She couldn't quite remember how she reached her parents' house in Midori, about three miles away, but there she collapsed from total exhaustion. Only after looking at herself in the mirror did she realize the extent of her burns. With a touch, her hair disintegrated into ashes, and when she washed it, her entire scalp slipped off like a cap from her head, leaving her completely bald. Her face, arms, and back were severely burned and on the oozing pinkish-red flesh her mother carefully placed freshly cut cucumbers. The availability of ample food, medical attention, and plenty of rest was what differentiated her condition from the others who perished soon after.

My sisters and I probably would have been sent to the countryside, like my cousins and many of the other children, and there we would have escaped the bomb. But nobody really escaped the horrors of the war. Nobody was left unscathed by the enormous suffering and tragedy caused by the bomb.

"I hate Americans," Aunt Haruko cried bitterly to me. "They took away my daughter and husband."

"Now, now," her younger brother chided her gently. "Don't say that. You should blame it on the war."

Many Japanese blamed their own government, particularly the military, while others, like Uncle Umetaro, blamed the Emperor. But all came to one conclusion: "NO MORE WARS! NO MORE HIROSHIMAS!"

Regardless of the effects of the war, I was convinced during my stay that my mother and father would have led a more fulfilled life if they had stayed in Japan. I was even more certain of this when my mother's brothers and sisters got together and thoroughly enjoyed each other's company. At other times, when I witnessed the ease and confidence in which my aunts and uncles negotiated their everyday lives, I began to appreciate how much my parents had given up when they left their homeland.

Many of their forgone advantages had to do with with knowing the language and being accepted, native-born citizens of Japan. In America, just going to the market was a challenge for my mother. There were times she bought toothpaste thinking it was shoe polish, or dishwashing soap instead of hand cream.

"*Nihongo dattara, nandemo yomerareru!*" She'd snap. That means, "If it's written in Japanese, I could read anything!" She was trying to convince her children that in her own native tongue she was very literate. Night after night, after finishing the evening meals, she would pull out her study book and practice her alphabets. Each letter had to be written perfectly before she went on to the next. But as hard as she tried, she never got beyond writing simple three- or four-letter words and signing her name. "It just won't sink in," she'd lament. "I'm too old." Mama was in her fifties when she started teaching herself how to write English.

Papa did much better with the English language. He had more practice using it with others, and he probably had a greater propensity for learning a foreign language than Mama, who was too embarrassed to practice her broken English. Because Japanese was the primary language spoken at home, Papa would teach the children English from an elementary school primer to prepare them for first grade. I'm sure that my mother was always too busy with chores to sit down and learn along with them.

When I was in Hiroshima, I often found myself in the same predicament as Mama, experiencing the same frustration and sense of helplessness. My cousin Shōsō-san would say an English word and ask me, "*Wakaru?*" ("Understand?")

"*Wakaru,*" I'd answer.

"*Wakaru?*" He would ask again.

"*Wakaru,*" I'd repeat, trying hard to hold back my irritation.

But when he'd ask for the third time, "*Wakaru?*" I would explode with, "I'M NOT DUMB! If it's English I could understand anything!"

On occasion, but seldom, being a foreigner can be to one's advantage like the time my sister, my daughter, and I boarded the bullet train from Tokyo to Kyoto. We had bought economy class tickets and had accidentally boarded the first class compartment of the train.

"My how spacious and luxurious," we commented to each other as we settled back to enjoy the ride. As the train started up, we thought it rather curious that our compartment was relatively empty. Where were the many others who were waiting with us to board the train? By the time the conductor came around to collect our tickets, we realized we had boarded the wrong compartment.

"You are sitting in the wrong section," he said in Japanese.

"What?" we asked in English.

"You purchased second class seats," he said pointing emphatically to our tickets.

"What?" we answered.

He grunted, waved his hand as though he were swatting a fly, then moved on to the next party.

Getting on trains, traveling to an unfamiliar place, stopping along the way to eat, asking directions, getting lost, none of these activities was a problem for my Aunt Haruko and Uncle Takejiro as we went to visit my mother's second eldest brother in Kuba, which was a thirty-minute train ride outside of Hiroshima City. Yet a similar itinerary set in America would have been enormously problematic and stressful for my mother except when she went along with one of her English-speaking children.

When we got off the train and started up the hill toward my uncle's house, Aunt Haruko spotted a beautiful lily growing along the slope of the train's bank. She decided she wanted the lily and so Uncle Takejiro obligingly found a stick and proceeded to pry the flower's roots from the bank while Aunt Haruko supervised the dig. I stood laughing, watching the nonchalant efforts of the two. In America, my mother would never think about doing anything so conspicuous in public out of fear that others might think badly about Japanese. One was always aware of sticking out and being the object of watchful, often hostile glares. Being an integral and accepted part of society was a great comfort and a way of life denied to my parents when they came to America. This to me was one of the greatest sacrifices they made when they left their homeland because their minority status determined the quality of their everyday lives, entrapped them into menial labor, isolated them in their small ethnic community, and cut them off from the rights granted to citizens of the dominant society.

As for myself, I felt as if I had come home when I first visited Japan. It was strange to see a sea of Asian faces come rolling toward me when the traffic lights turned green. But much as I felt myself blending in with the crowd, I guess I didn't.

"Notice how people stare at you wherever you go?" Shōsō-san pointed out. "They must know you're a foreigner." He looked at me askance, scratched his head, and grinned. "It must be the way you walk or dress."

My clothes were not significantly unusual compared to the fashions worn by the other women. My skirts may have been just a little shorter. We both concluded that it must be my walk and body language that gave me away, just as we Japanese Americans can instantly identify a Japanese tourist in America. My movement and gestures were just a little bit broader, my stride longer, my gait bouncier, my laugh louder, my look more direct than the native Japanese woman's. And for once in my life I was considered "big." After about a month in Japan, my sense of proportion and my self-image started to change as well. I felt big and tall. Standing at five feet three inches, I was relatively taller than the average Japanese woman and my feet were also larger. It was fun for a change to look over the tops of people's heads rather than to be buried below necks and chests.

I used to feel like a clumsy giant next to Shōsō-san's wife Takae-san, who was no more than four feet nine inches tall. I would watch her in awe as she busily moved from the storefront to the kitchen, to the parlor, taking care of customers, cooking, and serving lunch to her family. Is this what my life would be like if Mama and Papa had stayed in Japan, I'd ask myself?

Takae-san's daily routine started at five o'clock in the morning. She fixed breakfast for her husband and two boys, ages 17 and 16, who left the house at seven a.m. to catch their forty-five-minute bus ride to school.

No sooner would they leave than I'd hear, "*Ohayō! Okā-chan! Ohayō!*" ("Good morning! Mama! Good morning!") It was the parrot Lolita who eagerly waited for Takae-san to come and get her.

"Good morning, Rori-chan," Takae-san called out. "You're a good girl, aren't you?" She'd praise the bird like a child. Lolita would climb out of her cage and nestle her head on Takae-san's breast, closing her eyes and ruffling her yellow-green feathers about her neck as Takae-san scratched her head. When the ritual stopped, the parrot would bite Takae-san's finger and complain, "*Un, itai yo!*" ("That hurts!"). Together, with Lolita perched on her shoulder, they would descend the stairs to begin another day's work.

By eight-thirty, about the time I usually came down to eat breakfast, Takae-san's face would be gleaming with perspiration. A good part of her day had begun in the store, which was directly below their living quarters. Her work in the store included answering the phones, waiting on the customers, taking the orders, and keeping the books.

At about five p.m. she would wrap up her chores in the store and begin cooking the evening meal, which she served upstairs. After dinner, she'd lower the dirty dishes down a shaft to the kitchen and wash them before coming upstairs again with a tray of dessert, cold drinks, or tea, while all along Shōsō-san and the boys either watched television or attended to their personal matters.

Several nights when I stayed in Eno Machi, a mathematics tutor came over the house to help Daizo, her eldest son, with his studies. Before leaving, the teacher would sit in the parlor, in the seat reserved for guests, and quickly exchange light conversation while sipping a cold drink or tea and eating his dessert. I wondered how many nights a week he obligingly ate dessert and talked to parents who wanted to hear about their son's progress?

That particular night he methodically put eight chocolate ice cream bonbons into his small mouth and swallowed all of them in less than two minutes. He then quickly finished his coke, wiped his fingertips on a warm towel placed on a bamboo holder, gathered his jacket and briefcase, bowed politely, and bade good night.

After seeing him to the door, Takae-san would either iron clothes or busy herself with some other chores, staying awake until about one in the morning when her son, finished with his studies, turned off the light and went to sleep.

"Some of my friends don't sleep at all," Daizo said of his classmates, who were also preparing for their university entrance exams.

"That's the least I could do for my son to encourage him with his studies," Takae-san said. "It's lonely staying up by yourself." I wondered whether the mothers of those boys who didn't sleep at all did the same.

Although her life seemed hard in comparison to my own, I know that Takae-san considered herself quite fortunate. She had married into a merchant family that had been in the wholesale sugar business for ninety years. Although marrying the eldest son meant extra responsibilities, such as taking care of the in-laws and being the host for family events, it also had its rewards. Financially, she would never have to worry. Her husband Shōsō-san had inherited the family business and their eldest son Daizo would eventually take over when his father retired. Also, since the Sato family was doing quite well, Takae-san didn't have to live with her in-laws. Both Aunt Itsue and Uncle Umetaro had moved to Kabe, a thirty-minute car ride from the city, where Shōsō-san had built his parents a home. "They'll live longer in the countryside," he remarked, "away from the hustle and bustle of city life."

According to Aunt Itsue, every woman knew what it meant to marry the eldest son and therefore preferred to marry the second or third son. "The suffering and hardship to a wife of a *chōnan* [eldest son] are great," she told me. "She must make herself small and say 'hai, hai' [yes, yes] to the mother-in-law, never talk back, never fight with her husband. She keeps her thoughts to herself, shoves the words back deep in her throat because once they come out they vanish in the air and remain in the minds of others."

Openly speaking one's mind just was not done, particularly if one were a daughter-in-law. To maintain the general harmony within the extended family and to preserve one's sanity, a daughter-in-law had to find outlets to vent her frustrations or express her anger. Ebata-san, a neighbor in Kabe, took tea ceremony lessons as a means to calm her nerves. Pointing to her head, she confessed to me, "That's why I have *nurosa* [neurosis]. Because I keep everything inside."

She had extended an invitation for me to observe one of her tea ceremony classes and I gladly accepted. "Come tomorrow at ten," she said. I had suspected that something was bothering her when I first met her at Uncle Umetaro's and Aunt Itsue's house.

We were sitting on the sofa in the living room when a lizard, about five inches long, crept in through the open shōji screen. There in the middle of the room he stood watchfully gazing at us who were sitting on the sofa sipping cold drinks.

"Get me a broom," Uncle Umetaro calmly ordered his wife.

Aunt Itsue handed him the broom and held open the door as Uncle swept the lizard outside. Ebata-san went charging after the lizard who lay stunned on the gravel garden path and stomped on him with her *geta* [wooden sandals]. The lizard thrashed his tail back and forth desperately fighting to free himself, but Ebata-san brought her foot down harder, piercing his soft, silvery belly with the heel of her wooden *geta*. Uncle, Auntie, and I were rather taken aback with her ferocity in needlessly killing the creature, but we didn't say anything until she left.

When I met her at her house the next morning, the same tension and nervous energy engulfed her. She was dressed in a black kimono and for the first time I saw her with make-up: lipstick and a little blue eyeshadow. She was glad to see me. "My mother-in-law usually accompanies me," she said with a sly grin. "But since you're coming she's staying home today." Is that why she invited me, I asked myself.

As we walked briskly down the hill to Kabe Machi she chattered nonstop, through narrow streets, past a temple, and up a dirt road that maintenance men were repairing.

"I'm from Yokohama, you know. Living in the country, working in the fields, I've become a country bumpkin." Ebata-san turned into the gate and took her shoes off at the entrance where the tea ceremony teacher greeted us. She was a very delicate, small woman, her face rice-paper white with a stroke of red brushed on her small lips. I felt clumsy in her presence as we followed her into the room where eight other women sat, knees tucked neatly beneath them.

Ebata-san stood out from the rest in more ways than one. Approaching her fifties, she was much older than the others, who appeared to be in their early twenties. The worry lines between Ebata-san's brows, the dissatisfaction expressed in her pursed lips, the tension and sleepless nights shown by her hollow eyes, the honey-brown skin tanned from working in the rice fields were not a part of the young, white faces that nodded to acknowledge our presence.

I sat across from Ebata-san and watched as she proceeded with the ritual, whisking the tea into a frothy green foam. With a slight smile, she raised her head and offered me the tea. I was delighted with the "fragrant" aftertaste of the tea and surprised by the youthful transformation that Ebata-san had undergone. If I were in her situation, I would be taking tea ceremony lessons too, I thought. Ebata-san had learned how to cope with her situation. She had learned to *gaman* (to endure hardship).

Gaman was a word I had heard quite often while growing up. Mama and Papa used it frequently as an imperative, and the true meaning of the word was learned just by watching my parents conduct their daily lives. There was not room for complaining— one just learned to shut up and *gaman.* My older sisters had learned to internalize this concept and used it in their everyday lives, but its practice was modified considerably by the time it was handed down to me. In the words of my older sisters, "You kids are spoiled!"

The importance of the concept "to *gaman*" came back to me time and again when I was in Japan, particularly since I heard the word used frequently when people were talking about inter-personal family relationships. Much of this concept had to do with learning how to cope and to accept people and life conditions as they were. By watching how Aunt Itsue handled Uncle Umetaro, who was a very strong-willed, demanding, and stubborn man, I began to understand why their marriage was a harmonious one. She had learned to *gaman,* patiently listening to his complaints and catering to his needs. To fight back only created conflict. I discovered that the day I decided to walk to town and buy groceries for the evening meal.

"No, stay inside today," Uncle advised me when I casually mentioned my plans at breakfast.

"But I want to get exercise and besides I'll cook tonight and pick up the ingredients on my way back."

"Tell me what you want and I'll pick the ingredients," Uncle said.

"That's all right. Let me do it because I need the exercise—"

"Tomorrow you go together with Itsue. Today it's better you stay home." His persistence was starting to annoy me as he repeated, "Today it's going to rain so it's better you don't go."

The rain, that's what was worrying him so much. "I don't care if I get wet," I told him, hoping to allay his concerns. "I like the rain."

"No. It's better you stay inside."

Could it be that he's worried I'll get lost in town, or that something bad will happen to me? Or could it be that he doesn't want me to spend my money? "Okay, then I'll just go for a walk around the neighborhood," I offered as a concession. I was willing to postpone the grocery shopping just as long as I could step out of the house.

"No, stay home today," Uncle insisted.

By now I was extremely irritated. I could feel my face starting to flush and the muscles in my throat tighten. I wanted to tell him that I couldn't stand being cooped up in the house from the day before because of the rain. I had to get out. But my inability to express my feelings adequately in Japanese stopped me from saying what I really felt. It was clear from Uncle's rigid expression that the matter was closed against further discussion. His mind was made up. I was not to leave the house under any circumstances. (He never did tell me exactly why.)

I was searching for the right words to say but decided to remain silent after looking at Aunt Itsue, who was quietly washing vegetables. She was telling me in her silence, "Please listen to Uncle or there will be trouble." After accepting the fact that I would stay in, I immediately felt much better and the tension disappeared. Either I was to remain boiling inside from anger or succumb to Uncle's wishes, and it was far easier to do the latter.

I realized that my sisters were right about me. I was spoiled compared to them and probably to most Japanese women. It was difficult for me to repress my own wants and needs and not to say what was on my mind. I knew that I could never be as obedient and understanding as Auntie or as selfless and patient as Takae-san—not after being raised in America. In fact, after observing and experiencing the lives of women in Japan, I was never more glad that my parents had emigrated to America. I knew that I would never willingly trade lives with Takae-san, and I was absolutely certain that she wouldn't trade places with me either.

Both Shōsō-san and she couldn't understand how I, a woman alone, could leave my child back in America to come and study in Japan, albeit for six weeks. That I was divorced was totally beyond their comprehension. As Takae-san said to me, getting a divorce was unthinkable and getting remarried was almost next to impossible, especially if one had a child from a previous marriage. Takae-san and Shōsō-san both agreed that I should not tell the others that I had a child or that I was married. Many nights I lay awake worrying whether I said the wrong thing. In Japan, knowing what not to say was just as important as knowing what was appropriate.

Earlier, I had told Aunt Itsue that she was a good person, and she answered, *"Watashi wa baka dakara."* ("It's because I'm stupid.")

I disagreed wildy. She was compassionate, wise, considerate, and caring. She was like a mother to me and I loved her dearly.

Uncle Umetaro promptly instructed me that in Japan a compliment may often be an insult, or a person may say one thing but mean the opposite. I tried to explain to Auntie and Uncle that Americans are more direct, that if we like something or someone, we say so. Or course, it wasn't as simple as that, but the point I was trying to make was that I truly meant what I said. I suppose Uncle Umetaro was simply following the rules of interaction when he would say, *"Ah, dame!"* ["No good!"] each time I praised Aunt Itsue's cooking. As Aunt Haruko had informed me, people make fun of you when you brag about your wife.

Since I was faced each day with trying to decipher the true meaning of what people really meant to say, I soon caught on. But it was difficult at first.

"Ikinasan-na. Meiwaku o kakaru kara—" ("Don't go. You'll cause a disturbance"), Uncle Umetaro insisted. My mother's

cousin Harumi had invited me to dinner.

"*Soshite Harumi-san to amari kankei nai*" ("And you aren't that closely related to her"), Aunt Itsue reasoned.

"But why would she insist so adamantly that I come?" I asked.

"You don't know if she really meant it," Uncle replied. "People will say 'come over,' but whether they really mean it, you don't know."

"But wouldn't her feelings be hurt if—"

"I'm telling you, don't go. *Meiwaku o kakaru kara*" ("You'll cause a disturbance"), he repeated emphatically.

Did she feel obligated to invite me since I had made it a special point to meet her? Or did she genuinely want me over for dinner but didn't want to dominate my time and impose upon my busy schedule? Whatever the case, Uncle and Auntie were right. Harumi never did call back during the six weeks I was in Hiroshima. Perhaps her invitation was a polite gesture, just like we Americans say, "We must get together for lunch."

Meiwaku (to trouble, disturb, take up much of another's time) was a word that I heard used time and again, particularly when referring to nonrelatives or relatives not closely related. I worried often that I was causing *meiwaku* for Auntie and Uncle, and especially for Takae-san, when I stayed in Eno Machi. But never was I made to feel like I was unwelcome. The family took off from work, drove me to appointments, changed their schedules, just to accommodate my plans. I often worried as to whether I could extend the same kind of hospitality should one of them come to visit America.

Slight complications with my flight back to Los Angeles became a major concern that consumed the entire family's mind. My Zen Nippon flight from Hiroshima to Tokyo left me with only a half hour to catch my Pan American flight at four-forty-five p.m. back to the United States. With my heavy baggage stuffed with gifts and no one to help me transport it from one airline terminal to the next, they all worried whether I would be on time for my international flight.

Shōsō-san called to see if I could catch an earlier flight to Tokyo, but it was already booked.

Masahiro-san (Shōsō-san's younger brother) suggested putting wheels on my luggage; then it would be easier for me to transport by myself.

Takae-san suggested I run to Pan Am and get a porter to help me.

Aunt Itsue was convinced we should ask Uncle Takejiro to go with me to Tokyo since he wasn't working and could afford to go.

"If only we knew someone who's leaving on that same plane," Shōsō-san lamented.

"Don't worry," I assured them. "I'll manage somehow," although by now their anxiety had become my own. I knew the distance between Zen Nippon and Pan Am was fairly far, and on my flight in to Hiroshima, I hadn't seen any porters working the international flights.

Just as everyone was debating about what to do, a call from my sensei, Professor Wagatsuma, arrived. He suggested that I come to Tokyo and visit with his family a day before returning to America. Shōsō-san breathed a sigh of relief, but now he started to worry as to whether he could book an early flight to Tokyo for me so that I would have enough time to spend with Wagatsuma Sensei and his family.

A customer, who was listening to much of the discussion and had by now become very involved in my problem, offered to call a friend and see what he could do. "Many big companies book reservations in advance for their clients. Maybe my friend can manage something," he said, then left.

Less than half an hour later the customer called back confirming a space for me on an early flight out of Hiroshima. With that final confirmation and reassurance that Wagatsuma Sensei would meet me in Tokyo, everyone's worries were allayed. "Everything in Japan is done through '*osewa*' [aid, help, indebtedness] of another," Shōsō-san told me. "*Osewa* is what connects people with one another."

The *osewa* of others was what made the world go around in Japan, and *osewa* was what allowed me to get through each day.

But since I was an "outsider," many of the favors I received were based strictly on the obligations that Shōsō-san had accumulated over the years, and the indebtedness I was creating was really Shōsō-san's debt since he was the *chōnan* (eldest son), the main person responsible for me and my actions.

Though one of the hardest adjustments for me to make while I was in Japan was my loss of independence, what I found in its place was a tremendous sense of security. In many ways I was made to feel like a child, indulged, innocent, and thoroughly loved. My worries, decisions, happiness, and sorrow had become a family affair. This, I realized, was probably the greatest loss that my mother and father suffered when they left their homeland for America.

When I arrived at Narita Airport in Tokyo, Wagatsuma Sensei waited behind a roped area along with others who scanned the debarking passengers. "Sensei," I said, waving my hand to catch his attention. He looked right through me as though I was a stranger. He took a second take and grinned broadly. "I didn't even recognize you," he laughed. "You looked just like a Japanese girl." Sensei probably didn't know it, but that was the highest compliment he could have paid me. Nothing could have made Papa prouder.

10

A Family Reunion

*J*ust before Papa passed away, he had written a short essay and had submitted it to the *Hokubei Mainichi* (a Japanese vernacular newspaper distributed throughout northern California) for a writing contest. The general guidelines of the contest called for a person to write about his/her hobbies and to include those things that were the most important in his/her life. Papa's essay was chosen among the many submitted but he never lived to see it published in the paper. It read:

Meiro gyogi tadashiku yō iku suru koto	To raise children with cheerful and correct manners
Meishu ippon tsuri wo	One bottle of good sake and fishing
sōgo ryōkai danketsu ichi	Understand each other united in one
gimu o mamori ippan shakai ni yūgo subeshi	Be faithful to your duty; be in harmony with the society in general.

I have read this piece over a hundred times trying to better understand my father. The importance he placed upon raising children with good manners was readily apparent to me—it seemed like most of his waking hours at home were devoted to lecturing and disciplining his children to conform to codes of etiquette and proper thinking. His "hobbies," fishing and drinking good sake, also posed no surprises. Papa loved the fun and celebration that accompanied good *sake* (rice wine). And fishing was always more than just a hobby that brought relaxation and pleasure. It also meant survival, a way to feed his family. But the other points, involving the importance of understanding, unity, duty, and harmony, were rather puzzling to me, and after contemplating them for quite a while I realized that these facets of his life were precisely the areas in which he had the most difficulty matching his ideals with reality. Perhaps here lay the greatest source of his frustration while living in America.

Disharmony quite frequently reigned in our household because he had habitually let gambling come before his duty to provide for his family's financial security. As Kenji said, he was sure that Papa hated himself for not practicing what he preached, but he couldn't seem to help himself; his sense of self-control and duty were held prisoners to his addiction. And in terms of his wish to "understand each other united in one," I think he desperately wanted to be understood, especially by his children, but while he was alive and they were still young and living under his rule, they had rebelled, finding it difficult to reconcile his Japanese teachings with their everyday American life. It was only after his death when they could more freely pick and choose from among his teachings, that they would treasure those values and customs they felt worth keeping.

The kind of unity he wanted and foresaw never came to fruition, the kind where children adhere uniformly to parental authority and demands. But that our family still keeps in constant touch with Mama and with each other through letters, visits, special events, gift-giving, and by telephone attests to the psychological unity that Papa helped to create. Surely he would take some credit for the closeness he would observe between family members if he were to take part in one of our Christmas gatherings. Christmas was a special holiday for our family and for many Japanese Americans even if they were Buddhist. The festivities of the season, the joy of giving and receiving replaced the regligious significance of the holiday.

Once a year on Christmas day many of the sisters and their children make their yearly pilgrimage to Los Angeles to celebrate the holiday with my mother. That day is always a very special event richly packed with food, games, gifts, and plenty of holiday spirit. The hubbub steadily escalates with everyone busily talking to one another, catching up on all the gossip and changes the year has brought. The noise subsides only when the food is served and everyone digs into the array of dishes prepared by the different sisters. After the last dessert has been served and everyone is thoroughly satiated with good food, wine, and conversation, the Christmas caroling begins with the family all gathering around to harmonize our favorite Christmas songs that I have heard since the time I believed in Santa Claus.

Many of the sisters get misty-eyed, for the songs remind them of years long past when Papa was still alive and the family was very young and quite poor. But the joy of Christmas was never the property of the wealthy only, and poverty never seemed to dampen the spirits of my family. The sisters would gift wrap their own meager belongings and place them under the tree. Many times a branch from a cherry tree, decorated with a few handmade ornaments, took the place of a Christmas tree. The family would all sit down to dine on the fish that Papa had caught, then gather to sing the Christmas carols while eagerly looking forward to New Year's day, the only holiday in the entire year when nobody had to work and Papa was merry regardless of the worries he had.

My thoughts, and probably my sisters' too, would frequently turn to Papa when the singing began. Papa always encouraged his children to sing and thoroughly enjoyed the yuletide songs. It was only two days after Christmas that he passed away. During our singing I have often wondered to myself: What if Papa were to walk in the door this very moment? How would he react to the many changes that our family has seen since he had passed away? What would he be like if he were still alive today?

Maybe by now he would have accepted the Americanization that was rapidly encroaching even before his death, although I'm also positive that he would have fought the changes every step of the way. Divorce and interracial marriage would have been the areas most bitterly contested. According to Papa, marriage was a lifelong commitment, no matter how unsuitable the mate. It was a condition that was fated in one's life and could not be changed, just like birth and death. And marriage outside of one's race would have led only to unhappiness and divorce, besides tarnishing the family name and preventing the unmarried children from finding suitable mates.

Probably Papa would have attributed the divorces in the family to the independent and strong-willed natures of his daughters. Papa believed that a woman should be obedient and subordinate to men, that if she was too strong-minded and domineering she would never find happiness because men wanted to be the domineering force in their marriages.

"I told you so," would be his likely response to Yoko when she got a divorce. He used to predict sadness and doom for her because he felt that she was too strong-minded for her own good. "You should have been born a man," he'd tell her. "As willful as you are, you'll never make a man happy."

Another area that he would find very disconcerting would be the erosion of the hierarchical system. Perhaps his reaction would be similar to Keiko's when she first came to visit the family in Los Angeles several years after Papa's death. "I knew Dad's dream was to keep the Japanese traditions," Keiko told me. "All this obedience training that we had! And when I went home and saw it deteriorating considerably, I was appalled."

She cried the first night she arrived, upset by the way Hiromi and I were behaving toward Mama. In her mind we were very impudent and disrespectful. "You see, we were never allowed that luxury to talk openly to Mom or Dad," she explained. "My outrage was partially mixed with jealousy and resentment because you kids had the freedom that I had never known."

While Papa was alive, the children were not allowed to speak up to their elders and express what was on their minds. Although a sibling could be only one year older than another, she, by virtue of her seniority, could expect unquestioned obedience from the younger. And Kenji was given even greater authority than the rest of the sisters because he was a male.

"Go over there and massage Dad's back," he would order his younger sister Keiko, who complied until Papa dropped off to sleep. And although she was just as tired as Kenji after working the same number of hours in the field, he would order, "Kay, come over here and see what's wrong with my foot and massage it."

Keiko would think to herself, "Sure, you honor thy mother and father, but you don't have to cater to your brother and sisters too!" Although Keiko may have resented the arbitrary hierarchical system that prevailed, she also liberally applied its rules to her younger sisters, that is, until one day she was challenged by Midori. That incident vividly stood out in my mind since it was the first time that I had ever witnessed a younger sister defy the orders of an elder.

"I told Midori to do something and she didn't," Keiko recalled. "I stamped my foot down and yelled, 'You do it!' She looked me straight in the eye and stomped her *geta* (wooden sandals) right down on my foot and shouted, 'YOU DO IT YOURSELF!'" Keiko didn't quite know how to handle Midori's insubordination. She knew that she was being unreasonable in her demands, just like Kenji, yet she knew that the rule in our household required younger siblings to obey their elders.

"After that incident, I never hassled Midori again because I knew she wouldn't do what I told her," Keiko laughed. "Besides, I was ambivalent about my rights as an elder."

It might take some time to convince Papa that the sisters' adoption of egalitarianism and the acceptance of sibling equality had helped to resolve many of the conflicts of the past and actually had brought the family closer together. But undoubtedly, a greater disappointment that Papa might suffer would be the discovery that Mama lives by herself rather than with Kenji. Under the traditional Japanese family structure, the eldest son was expected to live with his parents and assume the financial and caretaking responsibilities for them. But after further investigation, Papa would realize that the decision to live alone was strictly Mama's. She has always insisted that as long as she was healthy and able to get around by herself, she didn't want to burden any of her children. And living alone has not meant neglect and abandonment, for the children continue to visit her weekly and to attend to her needs for care.

Despite the disappointments with the changes he would encounter, I think Papa would be pleased to learn that many of his nightly lectures were not "repelled like rain off an umbrella," but rather were internalized by his children as a wellspring of strength, especially while they coped with the larger society.

Papa knew that as long as we remained racially identifiable we would always be faced with racism and discrimination and would be associated with Japan. For that reason, he desperately sought to instill knowledge and pride about our cultural heritage. Many times he would admonish, "During my lifetime I hope that I can convince you that as long as you look Japanese, you are going to be Japanese. No one is going to say, 'Oh look, there goes an American.' And you may never see Japan, but everybody is going to say, 'There's that Japanese girl.'"

Papa's warning came to my mind when I took my son Greg for a checkup at the pediatrician's office. While waiting for his name to be called we sat in the waiting room along with a roomful of parents and their children. My son, who was almost three years old at the time, immediately started to pull out all the toys from the toy chest, finally settling on a big fire engine. Before long, another boy, about five or six years old, joined him in play, snatching the fire engine out of my son's hands and noisily cranking the ladder up and down. Greg marveled at the older boy's dexterity while opting for his second choice—a toy clock.

"Do you speak English?" asked the boy, and grabbed the clock out of Greg's hands.

"Clock," my son said, pointing at the toy as the boy rapidly twirled the hands on its face.

The boy let out a fearless yell jabbing his fingers within inches of my son's eyes. "Do you know karate?" he asked him. Just then the nurse called for the next patient and the boy disappeared with his parents into the examination rooms while my son happily retrieved the fire engine.

Papa was right. What he had warned his children about over four decades ago still rang true. My son had neither heard about karate, nor at his young age did he quite know the difference between Japanese and English. And although he is a Sansei/Yonsei (third/fourth generation American), he is still thought of by others to be as foreign as my Issei father.

As Greg started school and his contacts with other children increased, he became more aware of his ethnicity, reinforced by constant reminders from other children that he looked different.

"Chinese! Chinese!" they'd laugh, stringing their eyes up with their fingers to make their point.

"I'm gonna get 'im next time," he vowed clinching his small fists into a knot. "What can I say to hurt 'im?" he asked me.

"Who?"

"Josh!"

"What did he say to you?"

"He asked me what I am."

"Well, what did you say?"

"I'm from Mars. I'm a Martian."

"Why didn't you tell him the truth? Why didn't you say you're American like him and that your grandparents and greatgrandparents were from Japan?"

Greg listened intently. I suppose he thought he was better off being an alien from another planet than to be Japanese.

"Your ancestors have a long history, a rich culture. You should be proud to know who you are."

"Yeah! Josh doesn't even know where his ancestors are from. I asked 'im. He doesn't know!"

"Then aren't you the lucky one?" I asked. I knew who Greg was talking about. Josh was a very white-skinned boy with sandy-brown hair and a cherubic face. The chances were fair that if Josh was a third-fourth generation American, his parents may not know much about their ancestors either. Many Anglo-

Americans didn't know. That's what assimilation had done for them.

My commentary didn't seem to satisfy Greg, but several months later he came up with his own answer.

"Guess what Mom? These kids were about to make fun of me but I fooled 'em."

"What did you say?"

"I told 'em I'm Mexican!"

I knew I had a lot more talking to do.

Papa used to constantly remind his children about the cruel world that awaited them outside the family. He had concluded that as a minority, one had to rely on the favors and goodwill of those in power. In order to make a good impression and to gain their trust and confidence, one had to be accommodating without being obsequious, cautious and perceptive without arousing suspicion and distrust, assertive and direct without being threatening or offensive.

"The way a person dresses and grooms himself is very important," Papa would emphasize when giving his daughters advice on how to present themselves while securing a job. "A slovenly person who doesn't take pride in his personal appearance may never get a second chance because people make judgments about your abilities based on how you present yourself. You may be the nicest person in the world, and the most intelligent, but they'll never know it."

He would continue to exhort, "Listen carefully to what that person is saying. Don't blindly accept what he tells you. Be alert. Try to understand the unspoken word, the hidden motivations. Keep one step ahead of the other by reading his face. Listen to the tone of voice; observe his mannerisms, his facial expressions, and take note of what pleases him. And when it comes time for you to speak, be assertive. Don't vacillate. Let him know what you think and look him straight in the eye." Although in the Japanese culture it is considered impolite to look directly into the eyes of another while talking, Papa had probably observed that Americans associated direct eye contact with sincerity and forthrightness, that if a person could not look another in the eye, it meant that he or she had something to hide.

"Of course, always be appreciative of others," he would stress. "Anything you learn from others, any help that somebody offers to you, be grateful. You have to practice how to make people like you, to have them care for you, to make them want to do things for you."

One of Papa's favorite dinner lectures to his children dwelled on how they should behave if they were to receive company or to be the invited guests. Usually these lessons pertained specifically to Japanese customs. "If you go to someone's house and they offer you a dish of goodies, you might be famished but you have to say you don't want it," he would advise his daughters. "You don't just grab it and munch it down until the plate is empty." Playing the parts of both hostess and guest, he would demonstrate as he lectured. "If you are the hostess and serving tea, don't fill it up to the brim. You'll humiliate your guests, like you know that they're lower class. You only fill the cup about two-thirds of the way and serve it with your right hand—never the left! When you serve the rice, don't shovel three scoops into the bowls. Put *two* dainty scoops. Now if you are the guest and you should want more, nurse your bowl until there are two bites left. If it appears like your hostess is negligent and is not going to offer you more, just dally about and wait. Never eat to the last bite unless you are finished. And when you are finished, don't leave your dishes and take off! Stack them neatly, then excuse yourself."

If Papa were to attend one of our Christmas dinners and were served by his grandchildren, he might be appalled to find them filling his teacup to the brim, indiscriminately shoveling three or four scoops of rice into his bowl, and not serving him another helping because he still has two bites left. The cry of Papa's disgust would prevent the family from finishing their meal and properly stacking their dishes, but perhaps after a while his daughters would temper his anger by convincing him that they have passed on to their children many of the values that he had cherished.

"I tell my kids many of the same things Dad preached," Yoko

claimed. "I know they find my words unpleasant, but I say to them what Dad always said: 'If I didn't care about you kids, I wouldn't go through the trouble of saying these unkind words. I would shower you with kindness, shower you with goodies, and you'd love me for it temporarily, but what good would I have done you? Even if what I say is unpleasant and unkind, I want to be the one to tell you rather than you having to hear it as an adult from some friend or acquaintance. Believe me, it'll be very painful.'"

Mama often repeated, "Although Papa gambled and liked to drink, when it came to the discipline of his children, he was severe." Papa's strict discipline was the source of many conflicts in the family. All of his children feared him, some hated him and felt the family would have been better off without him, and some others idolized him, modeling their lives upon his ideals. But after his death, I think everyone would agree they were grateful for the strength and courage he had given them to cope with the many adversities they had to face.

Papa used to tell his children, "Don't be ashamed you are poor! Money is not the most important thing in the world. It is the strength of character and courage that you bring to life— that's what counts. If money is all you have to show for your life, then you are a failure and I am too."

If Papa had measured his own success by the strength and courage that he had given to his children, then perhaps he would have died thinking of himself as a wealthy man. Over the years I have watched my sisters deal with tragedy, death, and misfortune in their personal lives and have marveled at the strength and courage they have summoned for each occasion. I think all of them would agree that Papa's teachings helped them through their hard times.

Papa subscribed to the childrearing philosophy, "*Kuro o katte mo, sase!*" That is, "Make the children suffer, even if you have to buy it [suffering] for them," because through suffering a child matured and came to understand and appreciate life. Kenji agreed. "Our Dad gave us pain and suffering but those experiences made us stronger, people with pride and richness of feeling."

Mama also believed in the same tenet. She felt that it was only after coming to America and experiencing hardship that she had come to understand life. For that knowledge, she would be forever grateful to America. I had heard other Issei say the same thing as Mama, like Mrs. Yamaguchi who told me, "I didn't want to come [to America] . . . moving here and there, working hard, raising children . . . but if I stayed in Japan, I wouldn't have become human."

When I asked her why, her Issei friend answered for her very matter-of-factly, "Because she wouldn't have suffered. In Japan she could have done just as she pleased. Life would have been easy." Becoming "human" was not a quality innately bestowed upon a person from the moment of birth; rather it was an attribute earned through experiential knowledge, through hardship and suffering.

I suppose this perspective on suffering was a convenient coping mechanism to embrace, especially when my parents simply had no other choice because of their economic situation. Therefore, when it was pouring rain, Papa would say, "Let the children walk home in the rain. It'll make them appreciate school that much more." But in fact, nobody—Mama, Papa, or the older siblings—could afford to stop working just to pick up the children, when all they would get was a "little" wet from the rain.

Probably the greatest surprise awaiting Papa would be the changes that he would see in Mama. He would discover that without the constant pressures of financial worries, Mama could be the kind of companion he always wanted—charming, fun-loving, and witty. He used to blame her for his failures and accuse her of holding him back from making broader strokes because of her conservative and cautious approach to new situations. She was a convenient scapegoat, one who quietly accepted blame, catered to his mercurial moods, and uplifted his faltering ego with praise. But I think with age Papa would have come to realize that he was his own worst enemy and that she was the best friend he ever had.

What kind of relationship that Mama and Papa might now have if he were given the chance to grow old with her occurred to me not long ago when I was visiting my mother at her apartment. In the lobby of her complex I found her busily engaged in conversation with a handsome, elderly Issei man. They both turned to look at me as I approached with my son.

"Ah, is this your grandson?" the old man asked my mother who nodded proudly. "Such a big boy," he smiled, chucking him under the chin. He walked along with us as we headed toward Mama's apartment, and although he was walking with the aid of a cane, his stride was sprightly and his back was held straight as a sword. His tall stature and the stately pride with which he carried himself reminded me of Papa.

"You should go see the doctor. He'll tell you what's wrong with your leg," Mama lectured. He ignored her advice as she continued to harangue: "There're many doctors who accept Medicare. It won't cost you a cent."

The old man disregarded her comments. "How old are you?" he asked my son, who bounded ahead of us, sliding his hands along the wall railing.

"Did you hear me?" Mama exhorted. "Now don't be a fool. Go to the doctor!"

The old man nodded his head in agreement and disappeared into his apartment, probably relieved to get away from Mama's badgering.

"Who was that man?" I asked her once we closed the door behind us.

"Oh, a nice old man," she answered. "He doesn't know these things so I have to tell him. Instead, he just complains about his legs and suffers."

I smiled at Mama. In her older years she had grown to be very obstinate, feisty, and outspoken. Probably a lot of this quality had to do with the fact that she was allowed to be herself. Papa was no longer around to quiet her, to mold her personality.

As I was leaving her apartment and heading home, I came upon the old man again, hastily walking toward the mailboxes near the lobby as though expecting a very important letter. My thoughts turned to Papa once more. If he were still alive, would he have been like the old man and quietly tolerated Mama's scolding? He never did in the past, but I felt assured that he would have mellowed over the years.

Many of the problems that plagued their marriage would have been resolved by now. The pressing financial worries would have lifted once the children had grown older and become financially independent. And most of all, Papa's gambling would have subsided as the dens closed their doors during the late 1950s in the course of the Japanese American community's efforts to improve its image.

Before his death Papa did admit to Mama: "Without you, I could have never made it." Although he probably had come to that conclusion long before he told her, perhaps in his later years he would have grown to appreciate her even more, realizing that despite his claim to being the architect of the children's upbringing, she was undisputedly the foundation that kept the family together. And by now he also may have realized, just as Mama did, that after living in America for sixty-two years and giving life to thirteen children and twenty-three grandchildren, there is nothing left for him in Japan. America is home.

I could see Papa reclining on the daybed in Mama's living room, waiting for Mama to serve lunch: fresh-caught sea bass cut into thin slices and served on a bed of iceberg lettuce, hot *miso* (bean curd) soup, *tsukemono* (pickled vegetables), and steaming, shiny-white rice. I would be massaging his shoulders, running my palms over his bony back now brittle with age, as he drifted off in sleep to a time when his body knew no pain and he felt immortal and strong. Mama's constant patter would bring him back to the rhythmic pounding of my fists across his back. With his eyes still closed, he would talk to me, as a grown person, and I would listen.

"So you've been talking to the others about me, eh? Well, what did they tell you? That I liked to drink? Gamble? Did they use the same breath to tell you about my nightly lectures? Eh? Speak up! I can't hear you."

"Yes, Papa," I'd answer, not realizing he expected me to reply. Usually he talked and the children just listened.

"Well. Did it do them any good?"

"What?"

"My lectures!

"Yes, Papa."

"I knew someday they'd realize the value of my words." In a softer tone he'd continue. "Tell me. Are they doing all right?"

"Yes, Papa. Everyone. All eleven of us. We're doing just fine."

His muscles would finally relax, now rid of all tension and pain. "Can't say I left them any material wealth, but—"

"You left us your teachings. Kenji said that's worth even more because it's something we'll never lose. Something we can apply to our everyday lives."

"Kenji told you that?" Papa would smile with satisfaction. "What else did he tell you?"

"It's what he couldn't tell me that's still a mystery to me."

"Like what?"

"Your life in Japan. Your family. Your father—"

"That stinking bastard!" Papa's anger and resentment would resurface, fresh and raw. "Did Kenji tell you that I promised you kids would always know the security and warmth of your own family? Did he tell you that I promised I'd never abandon you children for others to raise? Did he tell you that?"

"Yes, Papa. He told me. And they were promises kept. You never left us. You're with us still."

Epilogue

"Mama's not there," Keiko said. "I brought flowers on New Year's day but I could tell she's not there." Keiko was talking about the grave—Mama's and Papa's grave.

"Why should she be in Liberty?" Hiromi reasoned. "She's been gone from there for thirty-four years."

They both spoke as though she were still alive, as though she had the power and will to be wherever she wanted—on earth or in heaven. It was easier to deal with her death that way.

Mama used to tell me, "It's not easy to die," and I didn't exactly know what she meant. But as I watched her body slowly deteriorate over the next nine days, I knew. Her kidneys failed; her lungs filled with liquids; her blood pressure dropped; the pain increased; we counted the hours. Around her bedside we rallied with outbursts of tears, pleadings of forgiveness, words of comfort and gratitude, and miraculously she would rebound.

Midori believed that Mama would have died months earlier if it wasn't for her anticipation of receiving the redress money that was going to be sent to the eldest first as a result of the Civil Liberties Act, H.R. 442 passed by Congress in 1988. She was anxiously waiting for the check like so many other elderly Issei.

"You have to let her go now," the doctor said to us. Mama wasn't dying because we weren't letting her. Despite the excruciating pain, she was holding on because we needed her.

"*Mada mada yo, Mama*" ("Not yet, not yet, Mama"), Hiromi reassured her. "Eh?" Mama answered loud and clear. We were stunned. Mama had not spoken a word since entering the hospital. Now we knew she still had the spirit to fight on. For a few more days she did, but on the third day she fell into a coma.

On her pillow I lay, listening to her breathing: loud, steady, mechanical, like a pump, her legs cold, her feet stiff and pointed like a ballerina's, her arms soft and warm still retaining the fever that ravaged her body throughout the day.

Keiko, Hiromi, and I sat watching, counting her every breath, her face a waxen pale yellow with not a trace of perspiration. The smell of death permeated the room, filled our nostrils, and clung to our clothes.

"Another one died," the nurse reported. "They always go in threes."

At five-forty a.m. on November 17, 1989, Mama took her last breath. The death watch had ended.

"I wish we had buried some of her ashes here," Harumi said. "This is where she belongs." In a sense Harumi was right. Los Angeles was where Mama had spent the last thirty-four years of her life. She considered it home. But in her handwritten will she requested: "Cremate my body and bury my ashes in Liberty." A place awaited her next to Papa. Mama would have had it no other way. She belonged with Papa even after death. Together their long journey would end in Liberty alongside other countrymen and women like themselves, who had left their families behind to brave a new world, to take their chances, to risk their lives for a better future.

Mama and Papa took with them a set of values and beliefs, a way of life, a time in history shared only with their contemporaries. With their passing, my only comfort came from the privilege I felt to have been their child, taking what I learned from them to share with the next generation.